Henry Montagu Butler

Public school sermons

Henry Montagu Butler
Public school sermons
ISBN/EAN: 9783337104917

Printed in Europe, USA, Canada, Australia, Japan

Cover: Foto ©Lupo / pixelio.de

More available books at **www.hansebooks.com**

PUBLIC SCHOOL SERMONS

BY

H. MONTAGU BUTLER, D.D.

MASTER OF TRINITY COLLEGE, CAMBRIDGE, AND FORMERLY
HEAD MASTER OF HARROW SCHOOL

LONDON
ISBISTER AND COMPANY Limited
15 & 16 TAVISTOCK STREET COVENT GARDEN
1899

TO THE MASTERS

LATE AND PRESENT

OF TWELVE OF OUR GREAT PUBLIC SCHOOLS

THESE SERMONS

PREACHED AT THEIR REQUEST FROM

THEIR SCHOOL PULPITS

ARE GRATEFULLY AND RESPECTFULLY DEDICATED

PREFACE

prompting each in turn to recognise its profound Christian responsibility to youth, to parents, to the Church, and the nation at large—this would have seemed scarcely credible in the boyhood of Mr. Gladstone, Archbishop Thomson, Archbishop Trench, or either of the late Sir Thomas Aclands; yet few would now question the fact. We have only to recall gratefully the names of such men as Arnold, Moberly, Vaughan, Thring, Benson, together with other names hardly less well known of devoted Assistant Masters, and the magnitude of the change is at once apparent.

I count it among the chief blessings of my life to have been on terms of close friendship with many of the Masters of our leading schools. To this I owe it that I have been not unfrequently invited to offer words of Christian counsel to the boys of those schools from the school pulpit. In responding gratefully to such invitations in many parts of England, I have always felt how much we masters had in common—the same delightful and constantly refreshing task of ministering to young minds and hearts, the same duties—essentially pastoral, though in different ways, whether for clergy or laymen—the same visible enemies

PREFACE

to fight, the same weaknesses and immaturities to strengthen, the same sacred Powers to invoke, the same privilege of linking the joyous aspirations of youth with the dream of active service to God and our country.

To consecrate youthful ambition to the cause of Christ and of those whom He calls His brethren is the loftiest of educational lessons. I am sure that its elements at least can be taught at school, and that the teaching, however imperfect, will be seldom quite forgotten and never despised.

Believing that the friends to whom this little volume is dedicated have long shared this conviction, and have done, or are still doing, their utmost to give it life and fruitfulness, I ask them to accept this slight token of deep respect and warm regard from one who never forgets that through many years of happy labour he had the high honour of being their "comrade in arms."

H. M. B.

TRINITY LODGE,
March 14, 1899.

CONTENTS

	PAGE
CHRISTIAN GREATNESS	13

Preached at Marlborough College on the Feast of St. Michael and All Angels, 1860

THE DEATH OF THE BISHOP OF CALCUTTA . . . 33

Preached at Harrow School, October 14th, 1866, on the arrival of the news of the death of George Edward Lynch Cotton, Lord Bishop of Calcutta

"SURSUM CORDA" 47

Preached at Haileybury College, October 19th, 1878

THE TRANSMISSION OF INSPIRATION . . . . .

Preached at Clifton College at the Guthrie Commemoration, 65
June 21st, 1879

EASTER DAY 81

Preached at King's School, Sherborne, on Easter Day, March 28th, 1880

"THE LEAST SHALL BE GREAT" 95

Preached at Eton College, May 23rd, 1886

"BUILDING OF OLD WASTE PLACES" 107

Preached in Sherborne Abbey, at the Commemoration of Sherborne School, June 25th, 1886

CONTENTS

	PAGE
"ABIDE IN ME"	121

    Preached in the Cathedral at the Commemoration of King's School, Canterbury, August 2nd, 1888

"LORD, AND WHAT SHALL THIS MAN DO?" . . . 137

    Preached at Radley College, June 29th, 1889

SONS OF THE HIGHEST 155

    Preached in the Cathedral, Winchester, July 12th, 1891

"STAND FAST IN THE FAITH, QUIT YOU LIKE MEN" . 171

    Preached at Wellington College on the day after the Annual Speech Day, June 19th, 1892

"FEAR GOD: HONOUR THE KING" 185

    Preached in the Abbey on Election Sunday, Westminster School, July 29th, 1894

THE RICH AND THE POOR 199

    Preached at Eton College, July 21st, 1895, for the Eton Mission at Hackney Wick

BLUSTER AND FAITH 215

    Preached at Rugby School, July 5th, 1896

PUBLIC SCHOOL *ESPRIT DE CORPS* 229

    Preached in the Parish Church on the Commemoration Day of Bromsgrove School, July 27th, 1898

IN MEMORIAM 241

    Address delivered at Harrow School, March 19th, 1895, in memory of Frederick Ponsonby, sixth Earl of Bessborough

THE ATTRACTION OF THE CROSS 255

    Preached at St. Paul's, Knightsbridge, during the London Mission, February 14th, 1885

CHRISTIAN GREATNESS

MARLBOROUGH COLLEGE,
 Preached on the Feast of St.
 Michael and All Angels, 1860.

At the same time came the disciples unto Jesus, saying, Who is the greatest in the kingdom of heaven?

And Jesus called a little child unto him, and set him in the midst of them,

And said, Verily I say unto you, Except ye be converted, and become as little children, ye shall not enter into the kingdom of heaven.

Whosoever therefore shall humble himself as this little child, the same is greatest in the kingdom of heaven.

ST. MATT. xviii. 1–4.

CHRISTIAN GREATNESS

THE question of the disciples was a very natural one, my brethren, and helps us, I think, to understand something as to the light in which Christ's teaching would at first appear to them. There was a time when the Apostles were not yet canonised Saints of Christendom, not yet honoured as writers of Gospels and Epistles. Probably at no time in their lives did the thought ever cross their minds that they would become so loved and venerated; but certainly in the early stages of their intercourse with Christ, they would all be deeply conscious that they were scholars, not teachers, very ignorant "disciples" of One whom they felt to be their Master, while apprehending most imperfectly His teaching, His mission, and His person. How often was He obliged to correct their crude notions! How constantly did they misunderstand the meaning of what He said! How incapable they were of distinguishing the earthly from the heavenly, rules from principles, the outward from the inward spirit!

Can we find a stronger—at this distance of time we almost say a stranger—example of this than is furnished by the passage which I have read to you from the Gospel of to-day? The chosen Apostles, the men who were called to be the foundation of the Christian Church, lived day by day in the blessed presence of Christ. They saw His deeds of mercy and of power. They heard Him speak of His heavenly Father and of theirs. They knew that He would sometimes continue all night in prayer to God. Every word that He uttered implied that He was acting for God and with God, in the very atmosphere of heaven. He spoke of a "kingdom of heaven," as a kingdom which was now at hand, and He strove by means of all the objects with which they were most familiar to make them see what was the meaning of this kingdom, how its principles, its laws, and its growth were different from those of earthly kingdoms. To all this they listened. It was addressed indeed mainly to the "multitude," to men and women whom they would regard as far more ignorant than themselves. As for *them*,

CHRISTIAN GREATNESS

surely they might by this time enter in some measure into the inner mysteries of this new kingdom of which they had heard so much. Their Master's heavenly life and heavenly words must surely have revealed to them something of the true constitution of that kingdom of heaven which every conversation, every parable, every miracle, seemed designed to explain and to illustrate.

And as a matter of fact what was the result? When they talked with one another as they followed Him in His daily journey, was it some difficult question of duty or of doctrine which they were anxious to have solved? Were they eager for the spread of their Master's kingdom, and painfully conscious of the worldly obstacles to be overcome before God's way should truly be known upon earth, His saving health unto all nations?

Was it some such problem as might have perplexed the inspired judgment of Paul, or might now press heavily on the mind of some English Bishop, or devoted missionary, striving painfully to lift the veil of darkness which hides Christ from a heathen empire?

No, my brethren, the difficulty of the Apostles

was a much simpler one. It was a difficulty to which little minds are subject even more than great ones. It was a difficulty prompted not by speculation, or by godly zeal, but by human selfishness. The kingdom of heaven was valuable not because God would by it subdue the earth and the evils that stain it, but because they would hold high places in it. The disciples were not ashamed to refer to their Master, whose every action breathed self-sacrifice, the question on which they had disputed by the way—Who is the greatest in the kingdom of heaven?

Brethren, have any of us ever said in our haste, "We can bear anything but misconception"? Has any one again ever had a favourite habit or principle which he has tried earnestly to recommend to others, and has found with bitter disappointment that they have utterly failed to apprehend it as he meant it to be apprehended; that they took its incidental evil and missed its essential good; that they so perverted and disfigured it by their selfishness and their blindness as to bring into universal discredit, not its originator, for that he could bear, but its very truth and beauty which he knows to be so priceless, and so capable, if rightly appreciated, of bringing men nearer to their God?

Is there any one, lastly, who has had occasion to lament that, in spite of all his efforts to influence others for good, to make them better and wiser and more in earnest, he can make no perceptible progress? That they seem always beginners, still unimpressible, still uninterested in all that is most precious? If there be any such in any society—and where is the society in which there are none?—let them think of what Christ's disappointment must have been to see those whom He had called to be pillars, tottering like reeds shaken by the wind; to find His beloved Apostles still so worldly; to discover that those whom He was training to preach His kingdom were discussing their own titles to precedence in it. Truly God hath chosen the weak things of this world to confound the wise. The divine strength of a cause is approved by the very feebleness of the instruments by which it triumphs. If for the moment it is painful to admit weakness in those whose perfection we now scarcely question, the pain is removed when we remember who was the source of that subsequent perfection, when the disputants became confessors and martyrs, and out of human weakness were made strong by the Spirit of Christ.

I have said that the question which the disciples put to Christ was a very natural question. They had been brought up, like poor men, to admire rank, and wealth, and power. They heard now of a new kingdom in which they were to act a prominent part. Surely it would have its aristocracy and its hierarchy. One man would be greater than another. In what then was its greatness to consist? Who would be the greatest man? Would it be the wealthiest? Or the most nobly born? Or the man of most winning manners? Or would it be the most eloquent teacher? Or the daring, impetuous, all-inspiring man of action? Or the rapt ascetic? Or the profound thinker? And who was the man among themselves to whom the palm would at length be given?

My brethren, is there not something infinitely sublime, as well as deeply touching, in the reply with which Christ rebuked and enlightened them? "He called a little child unto Him, and set him in the midst of them, and said, Whosoever shall humble himself as this little child, the same is the greatest in the kingdom of heaven."

CHRISTIAN GREATNESS

A strange paradox this. A hard lesson, which the world has not yet learned. Have we learned it ourselves? What is our standard of human greatness? Is it a Christian standard? I shall ask you to put this question to yourselves in a very plain and practical manner. If you will answer it with perfect honesty, we shall not in vain have dwelt together on the lesson suggested by the services of this solemn day.

Now we all have some notion of greatness, and it is well that we have it. Only the little disbelieve in greatness. We have all admired some persons whom we felt to be greater than ourselves. Perhaps we have our favourites in history, in poetry, in fiction, in politics. At all events, among our own immediate friends and companions there are some towards whom we feel instinctively drawn as by some powerful magnet. There is something in them which compels us to admire.

In rude ages of the world's history, physical force has been the chief object of admiration. The greatest man was the strongest. Is there, do you think, any parallel to this in a society like yours? Have you ever noticed that the largest influence was enjoyed by a boy who was known to be the strongest among you, or was distinguished for his superiority in games? Have you noticed how, on entering a room, he gave the tone to the conversation? How all hung upon what he said, and repeated it afterwards as something of acknowledged importance, something which others would care to hear? At such times you were unconsciously paying homage to one form of what you felt to be greatness. I do not stop to consider whether it was a high form, whether it deserved the homage it received. It is enough for the present to illustrate the manner in which the very youngest among us must own some standard of greatness.

Then again, in proportion as men become civilised, they learn to reverence intellectual greatness. Some persons are original thinkers. We cannot hear them talk, we cannot read what they have written, without feeling that they have richer minds than most men; that they understand better the true bearings of any matter which may be discussed; that they seem to penetrate by a kind of inspiration into human motives; that nothing ever seems quite new to them, armed as they are with a few luminous principles which may be applied to the solution of all questions however complicated and apparently novel. What a strange reverence we feel for those whose knowledge and judgment have been serviceable to *us*, those who have taught us to appreciate something good or beautiful which otherwise we should have passed over as commonplace and insignificant! And apart from any benefit which we may ourselves be conscious of having derived from it, how instinctively, how necessarily, we pay honour to intellectual power!

You all know well how this again is seen at school. It may be that boys frequently altogether lose sight of many intellectual gifts which older persons can discern and prize. At school, the gifts which are most readily appreciated are those which are most obviously tested by competition, and many of the highest gifts of the mind refuse to be tried by so rough a test. Here, it is the boy with the quickest memory, who is thought to be the cleverest, or the boy with the power of producing the largest immediate result with the least effort, or the boy who can catch most intuitively and reproduce most accurately and gracefully the style and the thought of an ancient writer. In later life we look far more for imagination, or for calmness and soundness of judgment; and many a boy who was laughed at for being dreamy and eccentric is acknowledged afterwards to be a man of genius. In short, the standard of boyhood is different from the standard of manhood, and it is well to remember that it is so; but the point here to be noticed is that boys no less than men do pay great reverence to what they consider to be intellectual power, not because they gain any good from it, but because it strikes them as something admirable in itself.

And, once more, who is there who does not admire what is called roughly "force of character"? Strong will, prompt and firm decision, even when unaccompanied by either a high aim or a matured wisdom, fascinate us and almost force us to approve them. There are so many idlers in the world, so many too who seem to be mere creatures of custom, that the sight of any one who acts vigorously and follows the bent of his own character is a positive relief. Almost everything is forgiven to the errors of a man of marked decision and energy. When a weak man stumbles, he finds few apologists. If we were asked suddenly to say what we meant by "a great man," we should probably find that the image which instantly sprung to our mind was an image of strength, of strength self-contained, independent, rapid, inflexible.

I have spoken of three forms of greatness, but the words of Christ suggest a fourth and a different one. In the kingdom of heaven, he that is greatest is he that is most like a little child. Childlike qualities are the main elements which make up Christian greatness.

We will glance at a few of these; but before doing so, it may be well to guard against a false interpretation which is practically often put upon Christ's words. In the kingdom of heaven there is a place for the child, but there is also a place for the man. The most childlike is the greatest, but he must not forget that the crisis will often come when he must put away childish things. The circumstances under which Christ spoke must be remembered. His object was to rebuke ambition, not to disparage firmness. He was not laying down a definition, but revealing a principle to those who had evidently been blind to it. We never find that Christ was anxious to guard His words against all possible abuse. When He said, "I came not to send peace but a sword," or "How hardly shall they that have riches enter into the kingdom of God," He could not doubt that many would misunderstand Him; but still He chose to lay down His principle in terms so peremptory that none could forget them, knowing that in the end wisdom would be justified of her children. We are sometimes disposed to dwell too exclusively on what we feel to be distinctively the childlike elements in the Christian character. They are so beautiful that we are almost tempted to demand for them an exclusive claim to Christ's approval. At such times let us remember that other utterance of inspired wisdom, "Brethren, be not children in understanding; howbeit in malice—or in evil—be ye children, but in understanding be men."

With this caution, let us give our unreserved reverence and affection to those characteristics of the child which, as our Lord assures us, make His followers truly "great."

First, think of the natural truthfulness of a child. It has been beautifully said of him, "He hath not skill to utter lies." It is not, of course, intended that many children are not sadly untruthful; that to conceal faults by lying is not one of the chief temptations of childhood; but still every one feels that there is something peculiarly unnatural in an untruth coming from a little child. A child

CHRISTIAN GREATNESS

cannot understand the disguises, the conventional phrases, by which he observes that his elders so often conceal their real thoughts. He does not pretend to admire in order to make conversation. He does not feign a sympathy which he does not feel. He is not fearful of uttering an opinion with which others will disagree. He does not feel his way before he commits himself to speak. In talking of anything which interests him, he tells us what he feels, and not what he thinks he ought to feel. And so it is with the great man. He hates everything underhand, everything like diplomatic intrigue. If he sees vice, he rebukes it boldly. He calls it by its right name. He admits no subtle sophistry to plead in its favour.

My brethren, have we attained to this essential basis of greatness, truthfulness, and its natural development—a jealous love of truth? Do we never make excuses? Do we never allow some dishonest evasion to be applauded or laughed at without protesting against it? Truthfulness is not the whole of Christianity; but it is sometimes spoken of as if it were something almost beside the Christian character. And thus many religious men have often failed to win respect for their religion, because it was manifest that they were stained by insincerities which the most worldly man can despise.

Truthfulness is one great characteristic of a child. Another is his sense of dependence. He has none of that pride which shrinks from owning obligations, and insists on standing alone. It is painful, fearful, to him to be left alone. He misses his father and his mother as the sources of his confidence and pleasures and pursuits. To win their approbation is his highest reward. To think of their will as harsh, to ridicule their authority as absurdly strict, would seem to him unnatural and horrible. Their will is his will. He and his parents are one.

Happy indeed, my brethren, is that boy who can pass from infancy to manhood, and thus think of his parents.

In the history of great men, what is more touching than their reverent devotion to their parents? The men whose days shall be long in the affection of posterity are the men who, in life, honoured their fathers and mothers.

Ask yourselves here again—let me ask the question for you—have *you*, in the sight of God, this indispensable title to greatness?

But you will see at once that the sense of

dependence which the child feels towards his earthly parents, is felt by the man towards his heavenly Father. To the man, it should be a fearful thing to feel alone in this world; alone in the dark; alone, with no heavenly voice to command, to suggest, to encourage. To be conscious of a divine and fatherly will acting with our own will, to distrust our own will utterly save in so far as it responds to the divine, to feel at unity with ourselves because we are one with Christ in God, this is the peace which passeth all understanding; this is the faith which overcometh the world; because the man who feels his entire dependence upon God exults in his entire independence of the world. This is the essence of the heroic character, to fear God and have no fear beside. To be energetic and decisive, to be able to command others, to inspire others with our will—this is not necessarily heroic. Do not ever be deluded into a worship of power. See how it is used. Is it used to God's glory, under a sense of a divine mission? Is it all given to Him? If not, it may be terrible, it may be tragic; but, my Christian brethren, believe me it is not great. The greatest man is he who feels most habitually his complete dependence on his God.

I will select but one more point in the childlike character, its purity, or innocence. We need not now perplex ourselves with the question when sin begins for the first time to act on the mind of a young child. The idea of childhood does, undoubtedly, involve the idea of innocence. Our Baptismal Service represents Christ as exhorting all men to follow the innocency of little children. Purity, innocence, what ideas they are! What a dark retrospect they open to our consciences! Yet it is something to feel still their holiness, something to bless God that there are others purer, more innocent, than ourselves. In speaking of men, the terms "purity" and "innocence" can, of course, be applied only with large deductions; but let them suggest to you this most precious conviction. In judging of the greatness of men, whether of those you see, or of those you read of in history, never allow yourselves for one moment to think lightly of anything that stains the purity of their lives. It is an abuse of literary power, it is treason to Christ, when writers can speak with hearty admiration of all that is impetuous and daring in the subject of their eulogy, while they speak of his excesses almost as a necessary phase in his character, deserving, therefore—nay, almost

CHRISTIAN GREATNESS

demanding—to be palliated as misfortunes for which he was hardly accountable. In searching for human greatness, never divorce from it the idea of purity.

My brethren, in speaking to you to-day about Christian greatness, I feel that I am urging on you thoughts which ought not to be without fruit.

We want more greatness in the world, more truth, more simplicity, more courage. If you do not have a true ideal of greatness, you will have a false one; and that is a falsehood which has marred many noble spirits.

The object of your education here—the object, more especially of that part of it which is connected with this Chapel—is to send you forth to live and die faithful to the principles which Christ approves. To admire greatness is natural and right. Oh, admire it far more than you do! But weigh it in the balance of the sanctuary. To apply a Christian judgment to common things is no easy task. If this Chapel shall, in after years, be associated by you with the instinctive belief that this task is not impossible—nay, that it must be done—the day of St. Michael and All Angels will for ever be to you a solemn feast-day. There is something stirring, quickening, in all Commemorations. They link the past with the present. They bid us hope for a noble future. Many already look back on this place as having been to them God's instrument for making them life-long servants of His Son. How many of you will hereafter do the same?

To-day the absent are present. To-day the prayers of many are passing up to God for *you*. For distance does not divide human sympathies, and death does not divide God's army.

> Part of the host have crossed the flood,
> And part are crossing now.

If there was anything in any one of them, known either by tradition or by face, that suggested to your minds an image of human greatness or goodness, ask yourselves, my brethren, whether it was not childlike in its nature; truthfulness in every word; conscious dependence upon God, manifest in every resolution and every suffering: a purity of heart, that spoke of peace within, of glimpses even on this earth, even amidst your common life, of the vision of the fulness of the holiness of God.

THE DEATH OF THE BISHOP OF CALCUTTA

HARROW SCHOOL,
Preached on October 14, 1866, on the arrival of the news of the death of George Edward Lynch Cotton, Lord Bishop of Calcutta.

C

Verily, verily, I say unto thee, When thou wast young, thou girdedst thyself, and walkedst whither thou wouldest: but when thou shalt be old, thou shalt stretch forth thy hands, and another shall gird thee, and carry thee whither thou wouldest not. This spake He, signifying by what death he should glorify God.—St. John xxi. 18, 19.

THE DEATH OF THE BISHOP OF CALCUTTA

I HAVE determined, not without some hesitation, to speak to you this evening of the great loss which the Church of England has just sustained in the death of the Bishop of Calcutta. Few of you, probably, knew even of his name, much less of his work; and, therefore, much of what I say may seem wanting in point, and be at once forgotten. But so it is with all sermons. We strike, here and there, some heart which God has already touched. Sometimes we let drop a thought or an expression which, scarcely understood at the time, is borne back upon some one's memory in later years; but, no doubt, the greater part of what we say is forgotten almost as soon as it is heard, or leaves, at best, a vague impression of more or less earnestness, more or less depth of feeling and conviction on the part of the preacher himself.

So with our present subject. I know in my own mind—and there are some at least here present who have even a better right to make the statement—that a most eminent and true-hearted servant of God has just been taken from us; taken, as we should all have presumed to say, "when best employed, and wanted most"; a man playing a very peculiar and much-needed part in the religious life of our times; combining in the highest degree gifts which it seems more and more difficult to reconcile—the practical sense and wisdom of the statesman with the ardour and simplicity of the ecclesiastical ruler; the free, fearless, unconventional love of truth of the layman and the scholar with the childlike faith and ever-deepening devotion of a true Father in God.

"Right dear in the sight of the Lord is the death of His saints." And it ought to be dear to us also, so far as we can enter into their characters. Let me, therefore, try to bring before you a few points which have struck me most in the work and character of this admirable man; and let us, one and all, pray to follow

DEATH OF THE BISHOP OF CALCUTTA

him, as he so simply and unaffectedly followed Christ.

Bishop Cotton was pre-eminently a Public School man. Had he died eight years ago, before his Indian career began, he would have been remembered chiefly as one who had laboured most zealously and most successfully for the spiritual welfare of Public Schools. He was himself—as I have mentioned once before from this place, when I was asking your help for the Public Schools which he was establishing in India—he was a member of one public school, an Assistant Master at a second, and, finally, the Head Master of a third. His life had been spent much with boys and young men. His heart was with them, and theirs with him. He believed in them—in their generous instincts, in their public spirit, in their powers of self-government, in their willingness to make sacrifices, in their outspoken avowal of weakness and difficulties. And, as he believed heartily in these high qualities, so he was very keenly alive to the dangers attending their spiritual welfare. Alike in the *Prayers for Public Schools*, which he published twenty years ago; in his *Introduction to Confirmation*, which was our text-book here within my own recollection; and in the *School Sermons* which he preached to boys like yourselves, you see the keenest and, at the same time, the tenderest recognition of what we all own to be our chief spiritual snares—fear of public opinion; a frivolous, careless spirit, getting root in a society of boys, and gradually eating out all generous love of knowledge, and of exertion, and of earnestness of all kinds; a low and worldly tone, independently of actual vice; a selfish indifference to the claims and the comfort of others; a mean desire for popularity; a habit of reading nothing but the most worthless literature; a neglect of the blessings of the Lord's Day, of prayer, of the Bible, and of Holy Communion. On all these points I know of no one who has spoken with more searching insight, and, at the same time, with more tender sympathy. It is the language, not of a strong man scorning petty temptations to which he has himself long been superior, but of a wise and loving father, making allowance for the young, doing full justice to their strength as well as their weakness, and earnestly, affectionately, for the sake of Christ, striving to save them from those infirmities which spoil and degrade so many youthful lives.

DEATH OF THE BISHOP OF CALCUTTA

I wish I could think that some of you were able to test the truth of my words by a knowledge of your own. In proportion as you knew his writings, you would, I believe, admit that what has just been said is only so far incorrect as it is altogether inadequate. And his writings seem to have a claim to be read here, partly because they have so close a bearing upon our peculiar life; partly because, from various circumstances, a very large part of his affectionate sympathy and regard was devoted to this place. Only a few months back he presented to our library his last two volumes of Sermons, dedicated as they were to his beloved College friend,* whose name our library bears, who preached his Consecration Sermon in Westminster Abbey, and had for thirty years shared and stimulated his zeal in every fruitful Christian work.

Of his influence as an Assistant Master at the great school to which the confidence of Arnold had called him, I will say only what I know, and much less than I believe to be true. His great success, and it was one gradually rather than suddenly attained, lay in the conviction which he inspired, that what he cared for most was the

* Charles John Vaughan, D.D., afterwards Dean of Llandaff.

distinctly Christian growth of his pupils. In certain subjects of intellectual teaching, especially in Divinity and in History, he had the gift of inspiring a strong stimulus; and he had far too much humour and geniality not to feel a hearty sympathy with the favourite games of his school. But his influence was not merely a moral influence, a healthy influence, a genial, invigorating influence. It was not of this vague kind. It was a Christian influence, or it was nothing. The springs of his own religious life lay very deep. He clung with all his heart to the Lord Jesus Christ. He had no idea of life, either for men or for boys, save as a cheerful, hearty sacrifice to Him. The words "our common Master" had a special force when coming from his lips. He was convinced, and always spoke and acted on the simple conviction, that in earliest boyhood, as well as in mature manhood, our Saviour could be zealously and efficiently served, and that every part of public school life, as well as of every other kind of life—life in the army, life in the medical or legal professions, life in the commonest details of business—could, without the slightest unreality or affectation, be dedicated as a sacred thing to Him.

DEATH OF THE BISHOP OF CALCUTTA

In this heart-deep conviction lay the secret of his influence, of his visible Christian growth, and of his ever-increasing cheerfulness; for I think it may safely be said that every year, while it made him a riper Christian, made him a more genial, a more animated, and, in every sense, a happier man.

It was doubtless the general belief in his matured Christian earnestness and wisdom that recommended him for the important work to which his latest energies in this country were directed. A great school had become disorganised. A new school had not yet found the secret of a healthy public life. Its moral and intellectual tone alike required renovation.

How, in a very few years, he was enabled by God's blessing to work out a thorough reform; how, by the weight of his unmistakable Christian resoluteness, he got rid of anarchy and stagnation; how he planted deep all the most generous aspirations of a public school; how he attracted to himself fellow-labourers animated by his own spirit; how he led them all, men and boys alike, by what was noblest and most unworldly in them; how he made them all deservedly proud of their school, and raised it to a pitch of efficiency not surpassed probably anywhere in England; how, lastly, when the time of his call to India arrived, he handed over to the successor whom he was himself allowed to nominate, a society fruitful in a promise which has since been more than abundantly fulfilled—all this is matter of social history, known to all who have traced the progress of public education in England, remembered most gratefully, most loyally, with deep affection, by some at least of those to whom I speak this evening. It was a great and blessed work, and nobly was it discharged; very calmly, very modestly, without any noise or parade; with that "quietness and confidence" which are the fitting atmosphere of all true Christian enterprises.

After six years devoted to this successful and happy labour, he was summoned to that greater work in which it has pleased God that his earthly life should be sacrificed. It was a most arduous task. To rule the Church in India; to meet the educated natives with sympathy, with respect, and with intelligence; to retain the apostolic love of souls, and of the poor and simple, which great office has so sad a tendency to chill; to stimulate at once and moderate the zeal of mis-

DEATH OF THE BISHOP OF CALCUTTA

sionaries; to command the respect of officers of the army, so numerous now in that reconquered land; lastly, and chiefly, to be a pattern of Christian simplicity, energy, and charity to all those Englishmen and Englishwomen who are so sorely tempted to see in India simply a temporary and unwelcome sojourn for purposes of personal gain;—to wield such an office rightly requires a rare combination, and a yet more rare maturity, of the highest Christian gifts.

How he of whom we speak bore himself in this great post I must speak but briefly, partly because my own knowledge is necessarily imperfect, partly because the subject could scarcely be made very intelligible or interesting to you. Suffice it to say that his wisdom and goodness were widely recognised; that his attempts to convey Christian faith to the highly educated Hindoos—that most difficult of enterprises—were respectfully welcomed; that the Charge which he delivered to his clergy three years ago, touching as it did on the most distracting questions of these distracted times, was a model alike of patient investigation, of Christian reverence, and of regard for that liberty wherewith Christ hath made us free; lastly, that one of his latest works, and one of those most dear to his heart, was that which we so recently brought before you—the extension to Europeans in India of the blessings of public schools.

And now this faithful Christian career is suddenly cut off by what we call a petty accident, just when it seemed most valuable. But he had never looked upon his life as his own. The verse which I had chosen for my text as applicable to such a life is, I have since discovered, that on which he preached his farewell sermon to the school which he had so successfully reanimated: "Verily, verily, I say unto thee, When thou wast young, thou girdedst thyself, and walkedst whither thou wouldest : but when thou shalt be old, thou shalt stretch forth thy hands, and another shall gird thee, and carry thee whither thou wouldest not. This spake He, signifying by what death he should glorify God."

A time comes, sooner or later, to all of us who are in earnest, when this truth becomes clear. We begin by thinking our lives are our own. We make our plans; we call them ours. But, if God deigns to enlist us in His army, and to separate us from the mass of triflers, He soon teaches us another lesson. He makes us fail where we ex-

DEATH OF THE BISHOP OF CALCUTTA

pected success. He gives us success for which we seemed but little fitted. He takes us from tastes and pursuits which were most congenial, and carries us whither we would not, giving us often a life which disappoints and a death which men call premature.

For such divine teaching this faithful servant of God was prepared. He went out to his distant work, hoping much to return, but prepared to die and see his friends no more. They, as they think of him, will talk, some of his transparent truthfulness, some of the rich sympathy and wisdom which made his letters so delightful a treasure—some of the sad impossibility of now inviting him to look on a happiness which his absence rendered almost incomplete; others, again, of his unfinished public work, and the blank which he has left in the foremost ranks of the Christian ministry. But he would have led our thoughts to higher hopes. He would have bade us all, and certainly not least the youngest, work for Christ, and live for Christ, and not be at all afraid to die for Christ; for that the service of God, whether on earth or in heaven, is the whole duty and glory of man, and that he who has been faithful over a few things here will be made a ruler over many things hereafter.

I will conclude with his own words, which some, perhaps, have heard before :

"Let us go forth cheerfully and boldly to our various spheres of duty, far asunder as they must lie, in the firm faith and persuasion that God's hand is over us, guiding and helping us to do His will; and that, though we cannot and must not expect to see all our personal wishes realised, though our callings must be widely different, though some must be in worldly things more prosperous than others, though we may not gird ourselves after our own pleasure, though we may and must indulge some natural grief at the thought that many of us will see each other no more on earth; yet, if we will obey One Guide, and listen to One Voice, we shall be safely brought together when our life's voyage is over, never again to be separated, never to wrong, or grieve, or misunderstand each other, never to sin, never to be tempted, never to know pain or sorrow, but to be holy and happy for ever in our Father's Home."*

* See the end of his *Marlborough Sermons*, 1858.

"SURSUM CORDA"

HAILEYBURY COLLEGE,
Preached October 19, 1878.

I will lift up mine eyes unto the hills, from whence cometh my help.—Psalm cxxi. 1

"SURSUM CORDA"

MORE than twenty years ago a wise and good man,* who had seen much of public life, declared that if he had to counsel young men, he could sum up all he had to say to them in one word—*Aspire*. And rather more than a hundred years ago, at a time of sore national perplexity, a great orator, at the close of a famous speech which some of you may know and admire, made this appeal to the House of Commons : " We ought to auspicate all our public proceedings with America with the old warning of the Church, ' Sursum Corda.' We ought to elevate our minds to the greatness of that trust to which the order of Providence has called us."†

* Sir James Stephen, K.C.B., late Regius Professor of Modern History in the University of Cambridge.

† Peroration of Burke's Speech on Conciliation with America, March 22, 1775.

My brethren, I cannot forget, as I stand before you to-day, that these noble words are the very motto of your famous school. If to others they are a trumpet sound, to you they are almost a gospel. Wherever you may be—you and the growing hundreds of your schoolfellows—in any part of the world, this thought of the uplifted heart, of the eyes raised to the eternal hills, should never be far from you. One might almost say of those two Latin words, and of the appeal that they make to the heart and the conscience, what was said of old to the people of God: "These words, which I command thee this day, shall be in thine heart: and thou shalt teach them diligently unto thy children, and shalt talk of them when thou sittest in thine house, and when thou walkest by the way, and when thou liest down, and when thou risest up. And thou shalt bind them for a sign upon thine hand, and they shall be as frontlets between thine eyes. And thou shalt write them upon the posts of thy house, and on thy gates."*

Will you suffer me to-day to try to show you how, by God's blessing, you may make your proud motto even more your own; how you can

* Deut. vi. 6.

"SURSUM CORDA"

carry about its spirit as well as its letter; how you can live it out in practice; how it may be near you when you need, to give you health and strength and a good courage?

I. We will think first of times of despondency. There *are* such times with all of us. They come to all hearts, even to the stoutest. There are moments when we expect to fail, not to succeed. We are not strong enough. We are not good enough. We are not lucky enough. We are too few, or we are too young, or we are too obscure. The mists lie thick about us. There is no outlook—only one low weary level, where all seems monotonous and commonplace, ready to choke and stifle all that does not breathe of earth.

Is this a state of mind that is new to any one? Let me show him by an example what I mean. There are two stories told of the boyhood of Nelson* which, to those who read them right, have a Bible ring about them. The first is when he was quite a child. He had strayed from his home, and was found a long way off quite alone. "I wonder fear did not drive you home," so they said to him when he returned. "Fear," he said; "I never saw fear; what is it?"

* Southey's *Life of Nelson*.

But now mark another and a different state of mind, when the young fearless child had become the sailor boy of eighteen. His health was broken, his spirits were gone. Years after, when he stood on the pinnacle of earthly glory, this is how he spoke of those dark hours. " I felt impressed with a feeling that I should never rise in my profession. I could discover no means of reaching the object of my ambition. After a long and gloomy reverie, in which I almost wished myself overboard, a sudden glow of patriotism was kindled within me, and presented my king and country as my patron. 'Well, then,' I exclaimed, 'I will be a hero, and, confiding in Providence, I will brave every danger.'" You know how that resolve was fulfilled.

Tell me, now, is not this a noble instance—an instance hard to forget—of *Sursum Corda* in hours of despondency? My young brethren, I advise you to remember it. How many a boy, even in this happy place, has said to himself, " I shall never get on at school. At home I was everything to every one. Here nobody seems to care for me." Again, how many a boy has said to himself, perhaps is even now saying, " I shall never rise in my Form. I have not the cleverness

"SURSUM CORDA"

or the quickness. While I am slowly coming, another steps down before me. Two hours with me often end in abject failure when half an hour with some more gifted companion ends in brilliant success."

So we say in fits of depression. Let those who please make light of them. I will never do so. I know school life too well. I would as soon have laughed at Nelson when he stood in his reverie by the side of his ship, and almost wished himself overboard. No, my friend, whoever you are, we will not laugh at you, nor yet will we counsel you to make too much of your trouble. We say to you, " Lift up your heart." Yes, in the name of God who made you, and gave you your strength and your weakness, in the name of human experience, in the name of the lives of hundreds of great men of whom the world of their day was not worthy, in the name of every chivalrous romance and every stirring ballad, in the name of the great school whose name you bear, and to whose high traditions you hope one day to add some broad stone of honour, *Sursum Corda—Lift up your heart!*

II. But does any one say, " Despondency? What is despondency? I never saw it." Are there any here whose hearts are mostly peopled with far other thoughts? Yes, my friends, in such a body as yours there must be many in whom there is no feeling so strong as that of hope, and on-looking, and eager forecasting. You are already shaping your plans for life. Is "shaping" too strong a word? Would it be truer to say "dreaming"? Let us, then, call it dreaming. The day-dreams of boyhood are often the waking dreams, the realised dreams, of manhood. I have little dread of such dreams. I had rather we dreamed more than that we dreamed less. Only in our dreams we should lift up our hearts. Over each dream should hover something of the vision of Jacob. You remember what the Bible says of it: "He dreamed, and behold a ladder set up on the earth, and the top of it reached to heaven: and behold the angels of God ascending and descending on it."*

"The top of it reached to heaven." In all our dreams let us try to have something of this.

In plain words, I would ask you, What *are* your dreams of the future? You, first, who are among the foremost scholars of your school generation, representing its industry, its refinement, its zeal

* Gen. xxviii. 12.

for knowledge, its love of poetry and of history, perhaps of some branch of science; and representing also its contempt for all that is slipshod, and pretentious, and vulgar—what, are your dreams of the coming time when these sheltering walls have for the last time closed upon you as Haileybury boys?

And you, again, who are foremost now in the games of your school; you who have gained what others are seeking for; you whose lightest word, whether you believe it or no, is so potent here for good and for evil; you who by weak connivance might allow the ingress of almost any unknown vice, and, still more, by strong co-operation, might expel it even if it were there already; you whose position is so assured, so secure, so enviable—what is *your* dream of the future? Is it to spend time pleasantly? Is it to pass muster with the average? Is it to do as others do—to learn more of the world, to be more at home in it, to echo its talk, to catch its tone, to breathe its air? Do some of you wish to hold your own in literary circles, and others in military circles, and others in athletic circles? Would this content you?

Then I say to you to-day, taking as my watchword the generous motto which you can never wish to disregard, "Lift up your hearts." Yes! lift them up in this great matter of the dreams of your youth. "Lift them up unto the Lord." Lift them up far above the vulgar level with which too many seem to be satisfied. If you cannot say with Nelson, "I will be a hero, and, confiding in Providence, I will brave every danger," say at least, "I will be a Christian; I will, God helping me, so live as not to forget how Christ lived. He did not live for comfort. Neither will I. When He passed His holy boyhood among the quiet hills of Nazareth, His dreams cannot have been of selfish distinction. Neither shall mine. I cannot follow Him in all that He was or in all that He did, but one thing I can do. I can dream of being good and of doing good. I can dread the bare possibility of ever being nothing better than rich and clever and popular and comfortable. That heaven of unchristian natures would be to me a hell. I should not find Christ there, and my dreams have been of Christ, and of those who are like Christ, even from my youth."

O my brethren, if God has already given you any of this exalted faith, may He for ever keep you steadfast in it. May all your dreams of fame, of power, of prosperity—and they cannot be too daring or too ardent—be linked always with dreams of doing good, of seeking truth, of being more than others are, of a righteousness and a usefulness exceeding the righteousness and the usefulness of the Scribes and Pharisees; of the bracing mountain climb, not of the lounge in town or valley; of the ladder reaching from heaven to earth—the labour, the suffering, and the helpfulness on earth; the blessing, the inspiration, the heart's treasure in heaven.

Try to believe me when I tell you that the dreaming power of these bright youthful days is one of the strongest forces that God has given you. Do not waste it. Do not fritter it away. Do not degrade it. Above all, do not pollute it. Lift up your hearts. Fix your dreams, set your affection, on things above, not on things of the earth. Make it your prayer that all who leave this place, and love its name, and cherish its traditions, may carry with them unworldly, ungrovelling, untarnished hearts—better than the average, more elevated than the common, knowing somewhat of the glory of the eternal hills, and trained to lift up their eyes to them for help.

III. We have dwelt long on this thought, yet if you will bear with me, we will follow it still a little farther. We will pass from the dreams of youth to the working time—shall I say the realities?—of manhood. As to realities, God knows which is the more real, the early dream or the later performance. Each may be true and each may be false. What I would now ask you to do is to travel beyond your own experience, and still to believe that all that is best in your school spirit may even then follow you. I want you to have some fairly clear notion even in these happy years of the trials and dangers of maturer life. Only within the last few days a voice, known and honoured here, has thus described some of the perils of our time. "The ignoble love of ease and pleasure; the degrading worship of wealth; the senseless extravagance of luxury; the effrontery of vice that, flushed with pride and fulness of bread, no longer condescends to pay to virtue even the tribute of hypocrisy; the low cynicism that sneers away all those better thoughts and higher aims that are the very breath of a nation's nobler life; these are some of the seeds of evil which, sown in our soil and by our own hands, may one day rise up, an exceeding great army, more to be dreaded than the invading hosts of any foreign foe."

"SURSUM CORDA"

My brethren, these dangers, which thoughtful men descry, may seem very far from you. I trust and believe they are. But if the famous saying of Wellington be true, that the battle of Waterloo was won on the playing-fields of Eton, so alas! is it true that these other "dishonest victories," as Milton might call them, are won but too often in the self-indulgent ways of our public schools.

It is because boys do not "lift up their hearts" at school in their work, in their notions of duty, in the forming of their companionships, that men do not lift up their hearts in after life in the merchant's office, in the clergyman's study, in the officers' mess-room, in the lawyer's chambers, in the Houses of Parliament. It is because boys learn early the fatal habit of swimming with the stream that men shrink in after years from the first mutterings of the storm and the first countercurrents of opposition or obloquy. Try to be now what you would wish to be then. If *then* you would of all things dread, as unworthy of yourselves and your school, the sordid, earthbound, unaspiring spirit, aspire now. "Lift up your hearts." Let none but elevated hopes be the hopes that you call your own.

IV. There is yet one other crisis when I would fain trust that our text may not fail you. I call it a crisis, and surely it is one, the hour of sore temptation to sin. There are times—who does not know them?—when, in the language of the Psalm, "our sins have taken such hold upon us that we are not able to look up." They keep us down like weights on a drowning man. They rob us of self-respect. They crowd in on our memories. They laugh at our good professions. They tell us we are hypocrites, unstable as water, at one moment eager devotees, at another captives "sold under sin."

These are moments of which no Christian would wish to speak lightly. They are times of trial, times when God seems to hide His face and leave us to ourselves, that we may learn that ourselves are worthless. They are the times of which the Christian poet * is thinking when he says in his prayer for Christ's ordained ministers:

> And O! when worn and tired they sigh
> With that more fearful war within,
> When Passion's storms are loud and high,
> And brooding o'er remembered sin
> The heart dies down.

* Keble's *Christian Year*.

"SURSUM CORDA"

Do you ask, can we even at such moments dare to offer our old counsel? Yes, we do. It is never so much needed. Then, too, in the name of Christ we say to you, "Lift up your hearts!" Lift them up even when they are unable to look up. Force them, by the strength of God, to rise above the low mists of sin and remorse. You will not find Christ there. "He is not there; He is risen." Follow Him in humble self-prostration, but also in sure and certain hope. Strike down every low passion, every enslaving habit; but as for your hearts, however bruised their wings, lift them up: lift them even to the Lord.

My brethren, I offer you these thoughts to-day in the name of our common Master. Take them with you, and sometimes think of them when, printed at the head of some school record, or stamped on some well-won prize, or blazoned over some well-known door, as if to hallow alike all daily labour and all exceptional distinction, you read the thrilling watchword of your school, *Sursum Corda*.

Take them as others who have been here before you have taken similar thoughts in times past. Of one such—one distinguished schoolfellow* of yours—one whose sudden and mysterious death has not yet faded from your memories, I have been thinking much since I came among you. I owe him much, and much of that debt is due to this place. He loved it with his whole heart. He felt a pride in its traditions. Whatever honours he himself won—and they were not few—he valued them, I believe, chiefly for your sake. When I was last here, here in this room, he was here also. We were rejoicing together at the completion of your beautiful chapel. When, a fortnight since, I heard of your great disaster, one of my first thoughts was how he would have grieved with you. And then I thought again how soon the building would be replaced, but how the tried friend would never return.

My brethren, that bright, loyal, unselfish life was not lived in vain. It drew forth love from many, reverence for simplicity, trust in friendship. And these thoughts are in truth some of the "things above," not of "the things of the earth." I can hardly wish you a greater blessing than

---

* John Henry Pratt, Senior Classic, 1872, Fellow of Trinity College, Assistant-Master at Harrow School, drowned in the Lake of Como, August 31, 1878.

that you may long continue to train such scholars, so modest, so unworldly, so true. So long as this blessing is granted you, your proud but Christian motto will not be put to shame. You will not be afraid of any evil tidings. Your heart will stand fast. Yes, you will lift up your hearts; you will lift them up unto the Lord.

THE TRANSMISSION OF INSPIRATION

CLIFTON COLLEGE,
   Preached at the Guthrie Commemoration, June 21, 1879.

E

And it came to pass, when they were gone over, that Elijah said unto Elisha, Ask what I shall do for thee, before I be taken away from thee. And Elisha said, I pray thee, let a double portion of thy spirit rest upon me. And he said, Thou hast asked a hard thing: nevertheless, if thou see me when I am taken from thee, it shall be so unto thee; but if not, it shall not be so.—2 KINGS ii. 9, 10.

THE TRANSMISSION OF INSPIRATION

IT is the closing scene of the great career of Elijah. The time of his departure was at hand. He would be alone during his last journey, as he visited for the last time one after another of the centres of sacred worship—Gilgal, Bethel, Jericho. At each halting-place he urged his faithful servant, Elisha, to leave him. At each the same answer of devotion was returned by the one man on the earth who understood him, and knew the divine secret of his greatness, "As the Lord liveth, and as thy soul liveth, I will not leave thee."

And now at last they stand together, these two great servants of God, the one at the close, the other at the beginning of an illustrious career. They stand together on the farther side of Jordan, the side of Elijah's native mountains, the sight of which recalled to him his earthly home. There they stood, and there the elder Prophet, with a touch surely of fatherly tenderness, addressed to his successor the solemn charge: "Ask what I shall do for thee, before I be taken away from thee." It reminds us of a yet more solemn charge, uttered on the eve of a yet more awful departure: "Whatsoever ye shall ask in my name, that will I do, that the Father may be glorified in the Son. If ye shall ask anything in my name, I will do it."

Elisha took his Master at his word. "I pray thee, let a double portion of thy spirit rest upon me." More accurately the expression seems to mean a two-thirds portion, an elder son's portion, that is, an ample, a munificent, a predominant portion, but not, in the strict sense of the words, a *double* portion. The prayer of Elisha at this great crisis is, not that he may be greater, holier, than his beloved Master, more faithful, more beneficent, more zealous, but that a large, generous portion of his Master's inspiration may rest even upon him.

What is the answer to this prayer? Surely most remarkable, however we explain it. "Thou hast asked a hard thing: nevertheless, if thou see me when I am taken from thee, it shall be so unto thee; but if not, it shall not be so."

None but those who have seen the Prophet as he is; seen him to the end; seen him when others lost sight of him; seen him in his glory as well as in his struggles; seen him as the accredited ambassador of God no less than as the vehement combatant among men; none but they shall inherit his spirit; on none but them shall fall the mantle of his inspiration. On all others the effect of his passage through the world will be but transient. It will pass when he too passes. He will impress, but not mould. He will stir the dry bones, but not re-create and re-clothe. He will elevate, but not inspire. The great Prophet passes from mortal view, and of the mass of men who once stood in awe of him it may be said, they go their way, and straightway forget what manner of man he was, and what manner of men they were as they listened to him, and as their hearts burned within them. Of a few men only—a very few—nay, perhaps of but one faithful friend and interpreter, can it be said with truth: In this successor the great prophet still lives and stirs. "The spirit of Elijah doth rest upon Elisha."

We have not time to pursue the story farther

or to draw out the contrast between the two servants of God. The spirit of the first rested upon the second, but how? Not in such a way as to efface his own self, to make him a mere faint copy, a feeble mechanical mouthpiece of his Master. To do this would be to impress, not to inspire. True inspiration crushes nothing, obliterates nothing, robs a character of none of its original and peculiar features. It leaves a man a man still; the same man that he was before; the storehouse of his gifts not rifled, the range of his versatility not circumscribed—only with the baser parts in him humbled and vanquished, and the nobler parts, his hopes, his prayers, his aspirations, his ventures, fired, fused, intensified, transfigured by the nearer touch of heaven.

Elisha did not repeat Elijah. If he had only repeated him, he would not have lived in his spirit. For Elijah was in the highest degree original, and no man who was not in a true sense original could have shared his mighty spirit.

But, now, has this story any message for us Christians? We feel something of its poetry, its majesty. Is it wholly a story of the past? Does it refer only to Prophets; only to the innermost circle of the great and the good ; only to unapproachable holiness, or extraordinary genius?

My Christian friends, I believe that it has a voice for you also. For what are you met here to-day ? It is your anniversary. What is it which you desire to commemorate ? Rich blessings received—patient sowing rewarded by ample harvests, a name already great and rapidly becoming greater, friendships, some holy and all delightful, examples high and animating, a spirit of brotherhood pervading your whole body, penetrating even to the youngest member, and making him one in heart with those who were your founders. All these are, as I have said, rich blessings. It would be easy to enlarge upon them, to draw them out in detail. In every great society there is always room for a reminder, like in spirit to that of the great Athenian orator,* when he holds up before his countrymen not so much the great deeds they have achieved, but the spirit which has prompted those deeds, the institutions which have nursed it, the habits and customs, the all-pervading tone, of which that spirit is at once the source and the outcome.

There is always, I repeat, room for such a

* Thuc. ii. 36.

reminder, and a day like this would be not ill-fitted for it. But then the speaker must be one of yourselves; one who has fought with you, and suffered with you, and conquered with you; one who has borne the burthen, and shared the misgivings, and shared also—perhaps inspired—the victorious faith; one who has been with you in those cold hours before the dawn which, while they try the nerve of the strongest, are the birth-time of lasting victory.

For myself, speaking to you as a stranger, I must speak less pointedly, less confidentially, but not, I hope, less earnestly. I would ask you to-day to look back upon all you have done, and look forward to all you yet hope to achieve, in the light of one great thought. Think of what is meant by the "transmission of inspiration"—the passing on from term to term, from year to year, from master to master, from boy to boy, from friend to friend, of that richest of all blessings which, with all reverence, we call the Spirit of God. Think what it is to have the power of bequeathing good, of founding virtue, of breathing into customs, institutions, genial intellects, grateful hearts, tender souls, a breath of life and energy which will never be extinct.

THE TRANSMISSION OF INSPIRATION

There is a noble passage in a famous speech of Grattan*—known, it may be, to some among you—where, pleading for his country's rights, he thus avows his faith: "Though the public speaker should die, yet the immortal fire shall outlast the organ which conveyed it; and the breath of liberty, like the word of the holy man, will not die with the prophet, but survive him."

He is speaking of the breath of civil liberty. I would ask you to think rather of the breath of earnest brotherhood, of manly diligence, of simple living, of elevated thought, of unsullied veracity, of scrupulous purity. These things, too, have a breath which it is the function of God's Prophets to inspire. Of them, too, it may be said that the breath does not die with the prophet, but survives him.

To foster, to keep alive, to transmit these sacred things, is the high privilege of Public Schools, from Winchester, justly proud of her five hundred years of fame, to your own great school on which still rests the dew of its youth. It is possible for these schools thus to transmit inspiration; it is possible for old and young alike, by labour, by

---

* Peroration of the Speech on the Declaration of Irish Rights, quoted in Appendix I. to vol. iv. of *Brougham's Speeches*.

patience, by faith in the progress of good, by closing the eye to no form of improvement, by fearlessness, by self-sacrifice, by love unfeigned, so to live here as to keep alive in all the conviction that a public school may be a temple of God. Nearly twenty years ago, when I first went to Harrow, I remember receiving a letter from a good and wise man* since taken from us, one who had had much experience and much success in education. He said : " The success of a school depends on the constant presence of the Spirit of God."

They are words which may be used lightly, conventionally, with little meaning ; but to minds "truly initiated and rightly taught" they "are in truth everything and all in all." They come back in times of apparent prosperity and times of apparent failure. They are the test and the touchstone of each. This praise that I hear, this blame that I hear, these forebodings that I hear : what is the one ? what is the other ? Is the Spirit of God still among us ? Do we still preserve the "transmission of inspiration" ?

My friends, for such creatures of a day as we

---

* The Rev. S. A. Pears, D.D., late Head Master of Repton School.

THE TRANSMISSION OF INSPIRATION

are it is a great thing to transmit an institution. In politics we think highly of the men who frame far-reaching statutes or found durable alliances. There are few nobler passages in political oratory than that in which Burke describes the great coalition formed by William III. during the last few months of his failing health to check the arrogance of Louis XIV.: "Just as the last hand was given to this immense and complicated machine, the master-workman died; but the work was formed on true mechanical principles, and it was as truly wrought. It went by the impulse it had received from the first mover. The man was dead, but the grand alliance survived in which King William lived and reigned."*

This is what we might call political inspiration—the work, under God, of the statesman or the soldier. But prophetic inspiration, of which we speak, is something yet nobler. It is the power of creating, not a great and complicated machine, but a spirit, a mind, a temper, a character. It is the power of founding, not something which is formed on true mechanical principles, but something which lives and moves and has its being in the heart, the emotions, the intellect, the conscience.

* Letter I. on a Regicide Peace.

Christian brethren, "covet earnestly the best gifts." Be ambitious of this noble heirloom, prophetic inspiration. Let each year as it comes, and as it finds you rich in expanding fame and accumulated triumphs, lead you to ask whether the old spirit is still breathing among you, whether all your aspirations are still heavenward, whether you are still in some true sense, which has not degenerated into a lifeless cant, doing "all in the name of the Lord Jesus"; whether the leaders among you, old and young alike, still look to the rock whence they were hewn and the hole of the pit whence they were digged; whether, in every department of your varied, your multitudinous life—in the chapel, the class-room, the bed-chamber, the playing-field, the council of the masters, the fireside chat of the knot of eager boys—whether, in a sense which God can approve, the spirit of Elijah still rests on Elisha.

My younger brethren, let me put to you one or two plain questions. I think you will understand me.

Have you ever thought of the inspiration of example, of the penetrating power of holy tradition, of what is done, and may always be done, by those who are in love with goodness, and, like

THE TRANSMISSION OF INSPIRATION

Elijah, "very jealous for the Lord God of Hosts"?

There are some lessons which we learn better on a small scale than on a vast scale; better by the experience of such a school as yours than by the study of the history of nations. No man, with his heart open, can watch over a life such as yours without feeling the mysterious, the divine, I will not hesitate to say the prophetic side of it. The power of noble example is marvellous. You know surely how, alike in a house and in the school at large, you can trace the effect of a bold, or a gentle, or a pure example. A boy leaves you, either by time or perhaps by death. He passes away, either into the outer world or the nearer presence of God, it matters not which, but he is still with you. His spirit rests first upon one successor and then upon another. The good that he did, the zeal that he showed, the timely protests that he made against the tyranny of godless or vulgar custom—nay, perhaps even more, the simple quiet beauty of his unselfish life —these things took hold of those, perhaps they were but a few, who saw him to the end, and who vowed that the things he lived for were the only things worth living for. Much that marked him has passed away and been forgotten, all that he simply shared with the mass of his companions. The commonplace part of him has gone, but the mysterious part of him—yes, the prophetic part of him, the part which carried him beyond himself, the part "hid with Christ in God," the part revealed, it may be, to but one or two companions who saw the secret spring of his goodness—this abides. This is the mantle which falls on the successor. This is that which makes us say, The spirit of the one friend whom we knew and loved rests upon others whom we have known and loved since, and on others, again, whom we know and love now. We will not ask which is the greater, which the lesser. It is the same Spirit of God that makes both so precious. "Like as the dew of Hermon"—high majestic Hermon—which fell also on the humbler but yet more sacred hill of Zion; "for there the Lord promised His blessing, and life for evermore."

May I hope that my meaning is not altogether obscure? Believe me, my brethren, I have seen much of public schools since my boyhood, and I tell you what I have seen and known. In every one of you there lies the power of leaving here, of founding here, before his departure, some good that will last, something that will, by God's help, inspire others, strike them as great and noble and beautiful, and therefore worth reproducing and handing on. It needs not to be on any great scale, much less anything pretentious or ostentatious. Best of all, perhaps, will it be if you are yourself unconscious of its spell. The most precious, the most penetrating parts of a character are often those which are most unconscious. Elijah did not think we should learn from his despondency. St. Paul could scarcely have expected to touch the hearts of posterity by his anxiety for the bodily health of Timothy or Epaphroditus. Those who strive to live pure, true, courageous lives may be quite sure that there will be at least a few who will be caught by the contagion of their purity, their truthfulness, and their courage. The mass of goodness will thus be increased. It will be easier for others to be good; and what higher praise could any one of us desire than that it should be said of him hereafter with truth : " He so lived among us and left such an example that he made it easier for others to be good" ?

Long periods of the world's history may pass before we see again such a Master as Elijah and such a disciple as Elisha. Nay, two great characters of that precise order will never again return. But that which gives their chief value to the lives of Elijah and Elisha is always possible. We can always, if we lean upon God and keep very humble, "speak the truth," "rebuke vice," and be "very jealous" for God's honour; and further, we can "make much of them that fear the Lord." We can admire and stand by the nobler spirits among us, not joining the triflers who laugh and criticise and would fain bring down all greatness to their own miserable level, but deeply honouring goodness, and seeing it as it is, not as it sometimes seems; seeing it wrapped about, not with the wretched mists and misconceptions of earth, but with the chariots of fire and the horses of fire that are ready to bear it to its heavenly home.

EASTER DAY

ING'S SCHOOL, SHERBORNE,
Preached on Easter Day, March 28, 1880.

F

If ye then be risen with Christ, seek those things which are above.—COL. iii. 1.

EASTER DAY

WE have here two facts, and an appeal founded upon them. The facts are, first, Christ has risen; secondly, you are risen with Him. And the appeal is, If this be so, seek the things above. The first fact is, I need hardly say, the joyful event which this great day records—a day dear to the heart of all Christendom, a day which in the West brings all true Christians to the Table of their victorious Master, and in the East, at least over the vast empire of Russia, makes each Christian greet each man he meets, whatever his rank, with the morning salutation, "Christ is risen."

Christian brethren, I shall say but a few words on this great fact, nor shall I attempt to argue. It is a great fact of history. It is positively true that Jesus Christ did really die upon the cross of Calvary, and that He did really rise again a few hours after, and did eat, drink, and talk with His chief earthly friends. You will find, as you grow older—some of you may be aware already—that many persons question this truth, and many, if I may be allowed such a phrase, fight shy of it. I am not thinking of those who dislike Christianity and are its openly avowed enemies. I am thinking of some of those who love and reverence Jesus Christ, and can hardly find any language too strong to describe His goodness and His wisdom. But they are not easy in their minds when His open grave is pointed to. They would be glad, if they could, to get rid of this and all other supernatural parts of the Gospel narrative. They would be glad to close the Gospels with the mournful scene of Christ's burial. Were it so, they think there would be less difficulty in recommending the Christian faith to honest lovers of truth. Many, they think, would believe in Christ Crucified who stagger at the assertion of Christ Risen.

Now, as I said, I do not propose to argue this great question. I would only warn you that it is a great question, and that the greatest possible results depend upon it. My own firm belief, increasing every year in firmness, is that a Christian Church without a faith in a literal Resurrection of

EASTER DAY

the Saviour is at the best a pious dream; that if you lay the axe to the literal fact of history, you deal the death-blow to the spiritual fact also; and that any so-called Gospel, based upon the theory that the Saviour rose in spirit, in power, or in appearance, but not in actual body and visible presence, is what St. Paul would have denounced as "another Gospel, which is not another." It is not the Gospel once delivered by Apostles and Evangelists. It is not the Gospel which has in part conquered, and is still engaged in conquering the world.

No, brethren, let us not be ashamed of our faith; and if any of us have lost it, or are losing it, let us at least not imagine that we are parting with a light thing and retaining all that we really need.

"The Lord is risen indeed." He is risen as He said. He has made good His own express promise. He said that He would rise, and He has risen.

But then, following St. Paul's thought, we come upon a second fact of a different kind. "Ye are risen with Christ." This language is constant with St. Paul. You find it in Epistles written at different parts of his life. You find it in the great Epistle to the Romans written before he left Corinth for

Judæa. You find it in this Epistle to the Colossians written afterwards, when he was a prisoner at Rome. It has become one of his favourite thoughts—that every Christian man has died with Jesus Christ and risen with Jesus Christ. He has shared the dying and the death, and he now shares the rising also. If you tell me this is a deep, a hard, a mystical saying, I cannot deny it. It seems to me certain that it is so. If you go on to say that, because it is mystical, it is also shadowy, aimless, unpractical, I must at once differ. I believe the thought is one of almost boundless power to those who can honestly make it their own, and are, so to speak, possessed by it. Let me ask you to try to follow me as I do my best to make it a little clearer. If St. Paul had been asked what the great event of Easter Day had done for Christians, can we not imagine him replying, What, know ye not that what Christ did once in the body He now does for each one of you in your spirit? By His dying He gave you the power of dying gradually, and at last being dead, to the power of your sins. By His rising He gave you the power of rising out of all your former corruption into freshness and newness of life. Such a Master makes His servants like Himself.

EASTER DAY

He acts in them. He lives in them. Of His fulness they receive. Only let them accept this high calling, and they shall see what He will enable them to do by the purification and transformation of their lives.

Thus, then, it is that St. Paul makes his final appeal to his friends. "If ye be risen with Christ, seek the things which are above." If you share Christ's life, share His thoughts, His interests, His aims. Away with all that grovels on the earth, with all that is low and gross and impure. That is not the region for a Christian. The Christian does not breathe his rightful air till he reaches the holy hills whereon his Master dwells.

And now, brethren, what counsel do you think St. Paul would offer to such as you and me if he could speak to us here this day? How he would lay hold on the facts of our peculiar life! How he would fix his eye, with sure Christian instinct, on all that makes it most itself, its youth, its freshness, its keen but friendly competitions, its vigorous training, alike of body and of intellect! How his spirit would kindle at the thought of its unity, its brotherhood, its close-knit membership! You remember how, when he writes to the Corinthians, with the remembrance of their brilliant Isthmian

EASTER DAY

would contrast with them the degrading things of earth! How tenderly he would urge them all to make their choice between the two, and in making it to remember their risen Lord and their own high calling of God in Christ Jesus!

Brethren, on this high Christian festival, with the vision of the Lord's holy Table not yet faded from our view, let us think of just a few of these "things above." Do not think of them as things beyond the grave, as things which some day may be given to you and other very saintly servants of Christ. Think of them as now existing, as the truest and best things that there are. If you like to say that the things above are the things of heaven, I find no fault with the word, but I would beg you to bear in mind that this heaven is acting with and mixing with earth. There is a "thing of heaven" in the cup of cold water, in the act of simple kindness, in the daily self-denial, in the curbing of a vehement temper, in the pursuit of worthy aims, in the loyalty to a noble cause. The things above—or, if you will, the things of heaven—are the things of the spirit, the things of the higher self, the things which God loves, the things which Christ by His example taught us to prize.

Some of you may have read in the noble daydreams of Plato of those eternal *Ideas* of which all that we see on earth is but the imperfect shadow—the real Good, the real Beautiful, the real True. These are, for those who can receive them, "the things above": high ideals to strive after through every stage of life, ideals which, to the Christian, have once been realised and for ever reconsecrated by the Perfect Man, Christ Jesus.

In truth, brethren, every honest pursuit that you can think of has in it two sets of things—the "things above" and the "things of earth." So it is in the great world, and so it is with you.

You know that this week and that which follows it are stirring weeks in the history of England. Upwards of a thousand gentlemen are striving together for seats in Parliament. What is a seat in Parliament from the Christian's point of view? What would St. Paul have had to say on such an ambition? What would have been said by a mightier even than St. Paul? Would it not be something of this kind? "In what you seek so eagerly there are two sets of things to be won—the things of earth and the things above." There is the gratification of party feeling, the rapture of victory, the social prestige, the local and national

EASTER DAY

influence, the proud consciousness of bearing a part in one of the grandest of earthly governments. All these things, even the highest of them, I call the things of earth. I find nothing here which would seem great to St. Paul or his Master.

But there are also "things above" which may well stir the pulse of a man who seeks for a seat in the Parliament of England. There is the longing to do good; the passion for justice and honour; the longing to save the lost, to reclaim the criminal, to educate the child, to break every yoke, to efface bitter feuds, to knit together estranged classes, to restrain hostile nations. There is the memory of great acts of justice and mercy which have been wrought in Parliament by the best men of former or of present times, by a Wilberforce, a Romilly, a Buxton, a Shaftesbury. All these things I call—and surely rightly call—"things above." God grant that the thirst for these things may be near the hearts of our countrymen in the coming weeks. God grant that when the time comes for any of you to seek such distinctions either for yourselves or for dear and trusted friends, you may enter on the struggle not as men of the world only, not as partisans only, not as men who keep their religion for Sundays and on six days of the week give their hearts without a struggle to the things of earth, but as pledged servants of Jesus Christ, as servants of a Master who has said, " My kingdom is not of this world," as pupils in the school of that great Apostle who has said, " If ye be risen with Christ, seek the things above."

I have said it is the same, brethren, with your world here as in the great world without. You have not yet your seats in Parliament to contend for, but you have your pursuits of all kinds which fill your field of vision up to its very horizon.

O let me counsel you, in all these pursuits keep the heart on the "things above." In your games keep your heart not on the personal victory, not on the pleasure of having beaten a rival, not on the prestige you win among your companions, not on anything that can be said about you, not on any of these lower things, but on the delight in first-rate excellence, in the pleasure given to your friends, in the healthy stir and distraction of mind, in the friendly school spirit which these games do so much to foster.

Again, in your school work, try to keep faithful to the things above, not to the lower things.

EASTER DAY

Think little of the marks, of the place, of the prize, of the scholarship, of the First Class, of the distinction in any of its varied forms, so well known to the members of this great and successful school; think rather of the delight in knowledge, of the beauty and fruitfulness of great thoughts, of the consecration to God and man of growing powers, of the credit brought to your school and parents. In a word, keep clear by God's help of all that is selfish. Self is that being of the past to which the Christian is ever striving to die, and to which the ideal Christian is already dead. Keep clear, I say, by God's help, of all that is selfish. Live you the life of those who have risen with Christ, and seek ever the things which are above.

And lastly, brethren, what we pray for each of you let us all join in praying on this Easter Day for the whole school. You know how different schools have their special motto. With one it is *Industria, Energy*. With another it is *Sursum Corda! Lift up your hearts!* With a third, that which is surnamed by the great name of Wellington, it is *Heroum Filii*, the *Sons of Heroes*. With you, brethren, whatever be your formal motto which you hold dear from long tradition, let the true motto of your hearts be *The things above*.

Let masters as they teach and maintain discipline, let the older boys as they help to govern, as they set an example, as they seek and win distinctions; let the younger boys as they enter into the spirit of the place and know as yet no higher ambition than to breathe the air of its best traditions, let one and all be true to the "things above."

Remember once more, there is nothing which has not its lower, earthier side. Games, competitions, teaching, school gatherings, even such ethereal things as grand music and moving chapel services, all these things have in them the self-seeking part, the part which God cannot bless, the part which earth has claimed, and annexed, and misgoverned, and polluted. But it shall not be so among you. Whatever your fortunes in the future, whatever the greatness or the trials in store for you, whatever your subjects of study, whatever your social traditions, you will remember the lesson of this Easter Day. You will remember that you are risen with Christ, and for His sake, because you are not your own but bought with a price, you will seek ever the "things above."

ETON COLLEGE,
Preached on May 23, 1886.

games full upon him, he says to them, "Know ye not that they which run in a race run all, but one receiveth the prize. So run that ye may obtain"; and if he could have seen and lived among the boys of a Public School; if he could have seen how they thrill with common pride and common regrets; if he could have marked the strange and mighty power that the whole society exercises upon each individual, and how, again, the faults and the merits of one do not end with him, but, in a measure, act upon all; if, in short, he had had before his eyes those mysterious facts of your daily life with which you are so familiar that I suppose you rarely stop even to think of their mystery, then do you not imagine that he would have found in the sight fresh food for one of his favourite and deepest thoughts, "We, the many, are one body in Christ, and every one members one of another"?

Speaking to such a body, and giving his heart to them, how would he urge them, for the sake of that Saviour by whose name they were called, and by whose risen life their spirits lived, to seek ever "the things above"! How he would dwell on the preciousness of these, the beauty, the dignity, the incomparable grandeur! How lovingly he

Then there arose a reasoning among them, which of them should be greatest. And Jesus, perceiving the thought of their heart, took a child, and set him by Him, and said unto them, Whosoever shall receive this child in my name receiveth me: and whosoever shall receive me receiveth Him that sent me: for he that is least among you all, the same shall be great.

ST. LUKE ix. 46-48.

"THE LEAST SHALL BE GREAT"

THERE is in one sense no difficulty in this passage—no hard words to be explained, no old customs to be explored. There is not one here, not even the youngest, who feels puzzled and perplexed as he listens. Nay, we feel we can, in a way, see the whole scene. It might have happened anywhere, at any time. There is nothing new in ambitious thoughts or ambitious dreams, either among old or young.

Not a day passes here without some of you, my friends, thinking, either as regards yourselves or your companions, Which of us, which of them, will be the greater? Who will win the prize which every one is most eager for—the prize in games, the prize in intellectual distinction, the prize in popularity and influence; some day, it may be, the prize in political power or social precedence? The thought, I say, is with us all constantly. You can see it in our talk; you might read it in our letters; anyhow you will find it in our hearts. Yes, I make bold to say, there are very few here present—just a few, perhaps, some too pure and childlike for selfish ambition, and some again too inert and sluggish—just a few who do not know what is here called the "reasoning of their heart," Which of us, which of them, shall be the greater? Most of us know it but too well, and we are taught it by illustrious masters.

One of your most dignified statesmen* and most finished scholars, who for seventy years loved this place with a boy's romantic love, wrote for himself an epitaph which is now upon the wall of your side Chapel. It was put there by his younger brother, Arthur, Duke of Wellington. I have myself spoken with the kinsman† who went with Wellington to choose the very slab on which the words are inscribed. The dead statesman and Viceroy there tells, in graceful verse, what he owes to Eton; and the first two words of the second couplet sum up all: "Magna sequi,"

* Marquess Wellesley.
† Hon. and Very Reverend Gerald Wellesley, formerly Dean of Windsor.

"THE LEAST SHALL BE GREAT"

"To follow greatness." That was his "supreme desire." But then what greatness? Here we pass from the school of the world into the school of Christ—from the presence of statesmen and orators and rulers into the presence of Him who took a child as the emblem of greatness. And now we come to the real difficulty of the passage before us. It is a spiritual difficulty.

Which of us, I ask, which of us, men and boys, feels the deep truth as well as the beauty of the surprise, the shock with which Jesus met the ambitious thoughts of His disciples? The outward act is plain. From the crowd around Him He took a little child; and as they gazed, He pointed to him, and said to them in substance, before they had time or perhaps hardihood to put any question, "There is your greatest. There is the answer to what I know is passing in your hearts. With me greatness and littleness change their meaning. If you would know who is your greatest, I will tell you. It is the least among you all."

What did Jesus mean? We can all, I think, dimly feel some part of what He meant, while not one among us will dare to say that he has fathomed anything like all. He must, I suppose, have meant at least this : That child stands for much that is most precious in the eyes of a Heavenly Father. He represents innocence, purity, truthfulness, and weakness. There is in him no cramping self-consciousness, no comparison of himself with others, no assertion of claims or merit, no duplicity of aim, no diplomatic stratagems. As the old German hymn puts it :

> He hath no skill to utter lies,
> His very heart is in his eyes.

And these qualities are just what God values, and what those who are taught of God gradually come to value. Nay, my friends, by this we know that we are Christ's disciples if we come to prize, as beyond all things else beautiful and precious, the simplicity and the purity of a child.

And let none of us imagine that this is an easy lesson. We live in a society in which almost everything about us says, "Try to be great, try to succeed." Histories and lives of great men are full of this lesson. Pictures, busts, and statues are full of it. Works of fiction, which shape so many dreams and are the real sermons to so many hearts, are always striking the same note.

"THE LEAST SHALL BE GREAT"

And more, the silent influence of friend upon friend, even of parent upon child, is full of the same lesson. It is taken for granted, as a kind of law of nature, that to shine, to win, to mount, to get higher and higher, is to be great.

And if we come to school life—which you will see is very near to my heart—why, its very atmosphere, if it could be analysed, is charged with the teaching, "Beat others, get knowledge of the world, prepare to be a man, get rid of the ignorances and awkwardnesses and shynesses which make men weak. 'To be weak is to be miserable.' Learn early, practise daily, the science of greatness, the art of success."

I do not think we exaggerate in using this language. I do not think any one of us, those who love our public school life most dearly, would say that it has any direct tendency to make us childlike and simple. It is not, it seems to me, public schoolmen who are likely to be the least startled by the Master's paradox, "The least among you shall be the greatest." No, I think it must sound to most of them a paradox, something, so to speak, in the teeth of what they looked for. Had it been said to them merely by some human friend, as his own or her own maxim, they would have set it down, almost with a smile, as eccentric and singular. But coming from Christ Himself, it refuses to be so set down. They accept it in a way. They say, "It doubtless represents a certain human ideal"; but it hardly occurs to them to ask whether it is not the very rock on which their own life has to be built.

This, then, my friends, is the thought that I would try, with God's blessing, to leave with you this morning. Christ wishes every school, every man and every boy in it, to value most that which is most childlike. Whatever thoughts you link with childhood—and they must be good thoughts —bring them to the interpretation of this divine picture, painted by Christ's own hand. As to the shining, the brilliant, the pushing and dominating elements of life, they can, as we say, take care of themselves. What Christ desires is to put honour on those weaker and more delicate elements which cannot take care of themselves, which need tender fostering and kindliest sympathy. I have always felt that the worst thing that could be said of any great school would be this: It drives the childlike spirit out of its boys. Many here must

"THE LEAST SHALL BE GREAT"

remember a passage in the great Greek historian* in which, speaking of a state of society terribly spoiled by party faction, he notes this one fatal symptom : "Simplicity, which is one of the chief elements in every noble nature, was laughed down and disappeared."

There are other evil spirits besides party faction which laugh down simplicity. If I were again a boy at school, I think I could bear the imputation of almost any charge rather than this : "You helped to laugh a young boy out of his childlikeness. You helped to laugh him out of his simplicity, his trustfulness, his love of truth, his love of home, his love of purity, his desire to be diligent and do his duty."

But if it is a base and a dreadful thing to laugh down the simplicity of childhood, it is a noble and a blessed thing to honour it. Have you noticed that Jesus Christ not only says that the unconscious little child is greater than his critics, and serves indeed as a model to them in the estimate of greatness ? He goes farther than this : He says, " Whosoever shall receive one such little child in my name receiveth me."

What do you suppose is meant by receiving one

* Thuc. iii. 83.

such little child? Do you imagine, any of you, that it refers only to poor, ignorant, neglected children—"waifs and strays" as they are called—children such as those to whom your Eton Mission in London so kindly ministers? God knows, the words have a voice that pleads for them, and such as them. God be thanked that in one great school after another that voice is being heard and obeyed. But you need not look beyond your own walls, and your own river, and your own playing-fields for the explanation of this great saying of Jesus Christ. Nowhere, I dare to say it, is Christ's appeal more plainly, more pathetically, urged than at school, "Receive this child in my name." Not only, "Take this new boy into your body. Make him one of yourselves. Teach him to catch your spirit, to be proud of you in after years, to enjoy the delightful freemasonry which, in every corner of the world, will find him friends and fellow-helpers, simply because he was once an Eton boy." All this has its charm. It has had it for years. All this was "said unto them of old time." But I say unto you, "Receive this child in my name, for my sake." Reverence his weakness. If he knows ill, shame him out of it. If he is loyal to good, help him to be true to

"THE LEAST SHALL BE GREAT"

it. Help him to believe, from the first day that he joins you, that no taunt against you would be so unjust as that of the unhappy Psalmist of old, "I had no place to flee unto, and no man cared for my soul." Help him, you that know this place best—all its greatness, and something too of its dangers—help him to believe that, just as the poet* says,

> The highest gift a hero leaves his race
> Is to have been a hero,

so the highest thing he can do for Eton, during the happy years before him, is to live the pure, unselfish, manly life of a Christian child.

"He took a child, and set him by Him." He did it once in Palestine. He does it here every day. We live among Christian parables. It is part of our greatness. Never did any teacher throw such glory round the weakness of childhood as Jesus Christ. And to no Christians, in no one part of the Holy Church throughout the world, does Jesus Christ say more audibly than to you, in the tone of a Brother, in the tone of a Saviour, in the tone also of a Judge: "See that ye despise not one of these little ones. Whoso shall

---
* George Eliot.

offend one of these little ones which believe in me"—ah! we will not now think of his doom. We will think rather of the fulness of the blessing, "Whoso shall receive this child in my name, receiveth me."

"BUILDING OF OLD WASTE PLACES"

SHERBORNE SCHOOL,
Preached in Sherborne Abbey, at
Commemoration, June 25, 1886.

Save now, I beseech Thee, O Lord: O Lord, I beseech Thee, send now prosperity.—PSALM cxviii. 25.

They that shall be of thee shall build the old waste places: thou shalt raise up the foundations of many generations; and thou shalt be called, The repairer of the breach, the restorer of paths to dwell in.—ISAIAH lviii. 12.

"BUILDING OF OLD WASTE PLACES"

WE listened, a few minutes since, to a stirring tale of restoration and of growth. The words indeed of the tale are almost studied in their naked simplicity, but beneath the coldness of the words you see moving a warm and vigorous life. This life is common to all great institutions, but with some it tells of a past struggle for existence, and even suspended animation.

Winchester and Eton have lived on continuously for five hundred and four hundred and fifty years, always Schools, never ruins.

Rugby, again, and my own Harrow spring fresh from the time of Elizabeth, when the "warfare" of the Reformation was "accomplished," and its work went on its way rejoicing. Neither school was linked with the old ecclesiastical order. In both the new life, religious, indeed, but secular, has flowed on for more than three hundred years without let or hindrance. But you, my friends, have had in a sense two and even three lives, with chasms between. You had the old life of the Cathedral and the Monastery. You inherit the new life of the school of the Reformation.

Think for a moment of something that was implied in that first sentence which was just read to us: "In the year 1550 King Edward VI. granted letters patent for the foundation of a Free Grammar School in the town of Sherborne, upon the humble petition of the inhabitants and others; and appointed certain lands, appertaining to the lapsed Chantries of the Abbey, to Governors named in the said letters patent for its maintenance."

In that phrase, "the lapsed chantries of the Abbey," how much is revealed! It needs far more historical knowledge than I possess to bring out the full significance of the words; but one thing seems fairly certain, that the year of your birth as a school was one of the gloomiest in the long life of England. It was marked by confusion at home and humiliation abroad. The Reformation had so far settled little and unsettled everything. It had swept away abuses and super-

"BUILDING OF OLD WASTE PLACES"

stitions, but it had not yet given us a purged faith and a reverent order of worship and government. "As to the mass of the people," so I read in the pages of one lay historian, not too much attached to the old Catholic Church, "hospitals were gone, schools broken up, almshouses swept away, every institution which Catholic piety had bequeathed for the support of the poor was either abolished or suspended till it could be organised anew; and the poor, themselves, smarting with rage and suffering, and seeing piety, honesty, and duty trampled under foot by their superiors, were sinking into savages."

That is one picture of the year of your birth. Here is another, drawn also by a lay hand: "Ecclesiastical order had come almost to an end. Patrons of livings presented their huntsmen or gamekeepers to the benefices in their gift, and kept the stipend. All teaching of divinity ceased at the Universities; the students, indeed, had fallen off in numbers, the libraries were in part scattered or burned, the intellectual impulse of the new learning died away." And then follows one more sentence which seems aimed at you: "One noble measure, indeed, the foundation of eighteen Grammar Schools" (of which you were,

I believe, the first) "was destined to throw a lustre over the name of Edward, but it had no time to bear fruit in his reign."

Such, my friends, were the birth-throes through which you emerged into your second life. The Monastery was swept away, with its pieties, its charities, and its culture, even as the Cathedral establishment had been swept away before it, and its place was to be supplied partly by its old Abbey Church, henceforward to be the church of a parish and a town, and partly by a school of which you are the latest, and one may well believe, the most privileged heirs.

For who can have listened to that long roll of Benefactors, each of whom has striven, in the grand language of the Prophet, to "build the old waste places, and raise up the foundations of many generations," without feeling that the last forty years, and not least the last ten years, stand pre-eminent as repairers of the breach and restorers of the path? None of your predecessors ever owed quite as much to Sherborne as "all ye who are here alive this day." You represent a new and vigorous life built up on the ruins of an exhausted and desolated past. When, near three hundred and fifty years ago, the Monks worshipped

"BUILDING OF OLD WASTE PLACES"

for the last time within these ancient walls, and then were driven forth to obscurity and contempt, how little could they have dreamed that, in the providence of God, the "breach" so ruthlessly made in old faiths and old homes would ever find a "repairer," and the curse be turned into a blessing!

But our work and your work is with the present, and, God willing, with the future. You stand, as it were, on the rebuilding of "the old waste places." Your worship, your studies, your music, your very games, are on the "foundations of many generations."

And what are some of the thoughts which on such a day haunt your minds, and would fain find some "timely utterance," however inadequate?

Let me take you for a moment to another great commemoration, even the completion of the restored temple at Jerusalem in the days of Nehemiah.

At the great service then held to God's honour at the Feast of Tabernacles, it is generally believed that the noble 118th Psalm was for the first time chanted. It is the Psalm, you will remember, which has verses like these: "The stone which the builders rejected, the same is become the head of the corner"; "This is the Lord's doing, and it is marvellous in our eyes"; "This is the day which the Lord hath made; we will rejoice and be glad in it."

And then those words which I chose for our leading text: "Save now, I beseech Thee, O Lord: O Lord, I beseech Thee, send now prosperity."

In that pious utterance of the heart and the mind, that Hosanna that looks both before and after and gives itself unto prayer, I find the best, the deepest outcome of our hearts to-day. Some will understand more than others the debt due to the past. Some, from their very temperament, will be touched more than others by what we call the *genius loci*, the thought of living day by day under the shadow of one of the most venerable of churches; but all alike will with one mouth swell the full chorus of affection and of prayer, "O Lord, I beseech Thee, send now prosperity."

And what do we mean by this word "prosperity," so lightly pronounced, so easily echoed, in common talk, on the cricket-ground, at the banquet, it may be even in the council chamber? I have often thought that, according as we interpret that word "prosperity" and all the gracious images that cluster round it, we test our own worthiness to inherit the traditions of a great public school. What, my friends, do you mean when you speak of the "prosperity" of Sherborne? Search your hearts a little. See whether any unworthy whispers have to be silenced before you arrive at a verdict that you dare to regard as final.

Does prosperity lie in numbers? Is China what you call a prosperous empire because she contains I know not how many hundreds of millions out of the total millions of the world? Is India more prosperous than Great Britain? Is the largest school necessarily the most "prosperous"? You would not care to say Yes to any one of these questions. At the best you would urge, numbers, and the public confidence that numbers imply, are but one element, and certainly not the largest, in the cup of "prosperity."

Well, then, is it intellectual success—nay, I will not say "success," I will say something better, intellectual zeal, intellectual enthusiasm—does this, when it exists, send us prosperity? Is all necessarily well with a school which possesses this great treasure? Is all necessarily evil with a school which possesses it not, or possesses it but little?

Here the question becomes more complicated. Intellectual enthusiasm, if widely diffused and long sustained, involves much that is more than intellectual — deep devotion on the part of teachers, loyal affection on the part of learners, a persistent faith on the part of both that the life is more than meat and even more than brain. Where such an assemblage of graces is found, prosperity will never be far off. And yet, I think, we shall hesitate to affirm that even in intellectual culture we have found what we are now seeking.

We want something which embraces all alike, the dullest as well as the cleverest, the strong arm as well as the subtle brain; nay, those who are neither strong nor clever nor in any way distinguished or interesting, and yet are English boys destined to be English men, and gifted each with a soul that will live on for ever.

Shall we, then, find this common link in the tie of brotherhood which binds all together, boy with boy, man with man, ay, and on a day like this, man with boy; yes, which knits together, on this day of commemoration, the hearts of all this crowded assembly as the heart—may I not dare to say it—of one boy? Is it here that you will find your much-prized "prosperity"?

"Largely here," is the answer, and yet not wholly here.

This proud and happy sense of brotherhood does not necessarily shut out—so experience seems to teach us—what is low and corrupting. *Esprit de corps*, though one of the most precious things of earth, is, after all, "of the earth," and liable to become "earthy." It does not exclude pride or indolence or worldliness or uncleanness. It gives to life very much of its charm, but it is not the "salt" which secures its purity. Without this generous passion no school can be prosperous; but in spite of that passion it may fail, or cease, to be prosperous.

Even so we have not yet found the object of our quest. No; if in this fair sanctuary of God we are to speak and think as in His presence, if we are to "rise up in His holy place," and send up to Him the thoughtful and the Christian prayer, "O Lord, I beseech Thee, send now prosperity," we must go beyond numbers, and beyond intellectual culture, and beyond even the delightful consciousness of being all members of one beloved and illustrious body. We must, as the Scripture says, "take hold on the paths of life." We must think of such graces as honesty, and truth in the inward parts, and diligence, and many-sided energy, and reverence for all that is lovely and of good report, and purity in word and thought, and simple prayerfulness, and that slowly trained unselfishness which, ever climbing, yes, climbing on its knees, reaches at last even the "shining tablelands"* and the pure refined air of Christian "love."

Brethren, let us, so far as we can, so far as each of us at present can, thus think of "prosperity": let us not be satisfied with anything that falls short of it. It would seem, from every sign that we see around us, as if the prosperity which has been so long granted to you "under the good hand of your God upon you" was likely to continue "for a great while to come." It looks as though with each quarter of a century you were destined to fill a larger and larger space in the heart of the country, and make an ever richer and richer contribution to its moral and intellectual life.

May it indeed be so! Even a stranger must

* Tennyson's *Ode on the Death of the Duke of Wellington.*

utter such a prayer with a full heart; how much more your own sons!

Only let the prayer be, now and always, all that the Christian's prayer should be—daring, aspiring, persistent, coveting earnestly the best gifts. Centuries ago these gifts were granted, often in high measure, to those who worshipped God and lived together in unity beneath the sheltering wing of this historic Abbey. They failed to use those gifts to the utmost. Some would even urge that they sinned them away. And yet they too in their day cared for the prosperity of Sherborne, and each month, as they fulfilled their course, they too, in the stately Latin of the 118th Psalm, chanted the Hosanna which is on our lips to-day.

Now, then, with the memories of the past upon us, humbling as well as cheering, and with all the bright hopes of a joyful future before us, let us, brethren, on this auspicious morning send up once more from this ancient house of prayer the spirit-searching petition to the Giver of every good and perfect gift: "Save now, I beseech Thee, O Lord: O Lord, I beseech Thee, send now prosperity."

KING'S SCHOOL, CANTERBURY.
Preached in the Cathedral at the
Commemoration, August 2, 1888.

Abide in me, and I in you. As the branch cannot bear fruit of itself, except it abide in the vine; no more can ye, except ye abide in me.—ST. JOHN XV. 4.

"ABIDE IN ME"

I HAVE asked myself how I could say something to you to-day, my young friends, which, by the blessing of God, might find a home in your hearts. You and I both know something of school life. We know its great happiness, its occasional troubles and disappointments, its grave temptations, its inexhaustible hopes. We ought to be able to understand each other and to help each other. Boys have always been my great helpers in teaching me the power and the sacredness of life. I have no desire to-day but to help you, if it may be, to make your lives very sacred and very powerful.

To do this, I bring you at once to Jesus Christ, and leave you with Him alone. He says, knowing what He can do for man, "Abide in me, and I in you." He knows that He can bring us through everything, and that no one else and nothing else can. All else, even the best and noblest of earth, fails the human soul in the hour of trial; but if we can "abide in" Jesus Christ, all is well with us. We are safe and strong ourselves, and, better still, we are like a vine, fruitful. We are strong enough to strengthen others.

Now how can we make such words as these to touch us with a living power, so that we really care for them, like the things of which we think and talk and dream?

We must bring them into the presence of our actual life here, that life which we know so well, and which we prize so keenly. We must "abide in Christ" by striving after the mind of Christ, and doing the things which He wishes us to do here. What are some of those things?

I will begin by saying, Kindness to each other. Just thirty years ago a very illustrious Canon of Canterbury,* a man greatly beloved, was preaching in this place to the boys of this school. He used these strong words. As I repeat them, ask yourselves, from your knowledge of this place, whether they seem to you too strong to be true.

"There is," he says, "no class where Christ can

* Arthur Penrhyn Stanley, D.D., afterwards Dean of Westminster.

be so faithfully served, or so cruelly persecuted, in the persons of His little ones, as amongst boys at school." And again he says, he, one of the most chivalrous friends who ever lived, never perhaps quite happy unless the cause for which he was contending was despised and unpopular: "The duty—the privilege, let me rather call it—of protecting the weak, of saving the innocent, of guiding the doubtful, of keeping down and driving away the tempter and the persecutor, this is, or ought to be, the very religion of schoolboys."

Yes, chivalry, rightly understood, is indeed the very religion of schoolboys, the grace by virtue of which they "abide in" Jesus Christ. As I say this, my young friends, don't misunderstand me. Don't carry your minds off to imaginary cases of gross bullying. Such cases are rare indeed in our modern school life. No such case, I feel quite sure, is troubling the heart of any boy here to-day. But, as you know, cases occur daily at school where a little kindness, or a little unkindness, makes all the difference in a young boy's happiness. It is sometimes said, in a shallow conventional way, boys go to school to "rough it," to "have their nonsense knocked out of them," to "rub off angularities," and the like. You know as well as I do the phrases that are used to express this supposed blessing of replacing softness by hardness, something which yields by something which will wear.

You must not expect me to echo or sanction such phrases. Of course I can see a certain grain of truth in them. But they are far indeed from expressing my experience of school life. I would, if I could, have far less roughness. I believe that manliness is taught not by roughness but by sympathy. I believe that, if you wish to make boys manly, you must hold up before them in an attractive way something daring to contend for, something precious to give up, something beautiful to win. You must make the least of their weaknesses and the most of their strength. You must laugh at nothing in them, certainly not their scruples, or their religious habits, or their purity; to laugh at those is, indeed, devil's work; but, more than this, you must not laugh at their nervousness, or their shyness and awkwardness, or even what looks like their cowardice.

Let me tell you here a beautiful story of one of our purest naval heroes. Every one knows something of Nelson, but it is not every one who knows anything of the man whom Nelson called his "right arm," I mean Sir Alexander Ball. This is the testimony borne to him in later life by another distinguished officer * : "Sir Alexander," he said, "has, I daresay, forgotten the circumstance; but, when he was Lieutenant Ball, he was the officer whom I accompanied in my first boat expedition, being then a midshipman, and only in my fourteenth year.

"As we were rowing up to the vessel which we were to attack, amid a discharge of musquetry, I was overpowered by fear; my knees trembled under me, and I seemed on the point of fainting away. Lieutenant Ball . . . placed himself close beside me, and still keeping his face directed toward the enemy, took hold of my hand, and pressing it in the most friendly manner, said in a low voice, 'Courage, my dear boy! Don't be afraid of yourself! You will recover in a minute or two. *I* was just the same when I first went out in this way.'

"Sir," said the officer to the friend to whom he was telling this story, "it was as if an angel had put a new soul into me. With the feeling that I was not yet dishonoured, the whole burthen of

* See S. T. Coleridge's *The Friend*, vol. iii. p. 231.

agony was removed; and from that moment I was as fearless and forward as the oldest of the boat's crew, and on our return the Lieutenant spoke highly of me to our Captain. I am scarcely less convinced of my own being than that I should have been what I tremble to think of if, instead of his humane encouragement, he had at that moment scoffed, threatened, or reviled me."

My young friends, forget, if you like, everything else I have said to you, but don't forget that story. It is a sort of parable of school life—of all life in a sense, but of school life specially. Be kind to all who need kindness, and who does not? Never laugh at weakness. Never gloat over seeing boy or man at his worst. Never recall to any one, with a sneer, the meanest or the feeblest moments of his life, but only the bravest and the purest. And never doubt that over all such deeds and such forbearances as that to which you have just listened there hangs inscribed a more than human praise. It is of such deeds that, as we listen, we hear, with beating hearts, two voices. One of them is that of the human narrator, and the other—I would say it with reverence—is the voice of Him who can nowhere be more truly served than by kindness and chivalry at school:

"ABIDE IN ME"

"Inasmuch as ye have done it—inasmuch as thou hast done it, unto one of the least of these, my brethren, ye have done it, thou, even thou, hast done it, unto me."

Kindness is one part of the mind of Christ by which during our school days we may "abide in Him."

Another is, to have high aims. An admirable man,* speaking some thirty-five years ago to an assembly of young men, told them that he could sum all that he had to say to them in one word—*Aspire*.

Now observe, as we listen to this word we are not necessarily brought nearer to Christ. The word may stir, and shake, and kindle dormant ambitions and energies, but it may well be that the Lord is not in the wind or the earthquake or even in the fire. To aspire, no doubt, is something; nay, it is much. Anything better, young boys, than lounging through life, or grovelling amid low contentments, or wallowing among sensual indulgences. Anything better than that.

To aspire, I repeat, is much. But here, assembled in this great sanctuary of the God of the Christian,

---

* Sir James Stephen, Professor of Modern History in the University of Cambridge.

we are not content with simple aspiration. Here we desire to "abide in Christ"; to keep with Him as we mount; and, when we "lift up our hearts" to whatever things are lofty, or pure, or lovely, or dangerous, or beneficent, or heroic, to lift them up to Him.

The life of Jesus Christ—has this sufficiently struck you?—was one of constant aspiration, of aiming at the highest. "Lifting up His eyes unto heaven," of which we hear in the great seventeenth chapter of St. John, is but a type of a constant mental attitude. The Man of Sorrows had ever a mighty joy set before Him—the joy of saving, of winning, of finding the lost, of cleansing the unclean, of answering the cry of troubled swelling hearts, of bringing many sons and many daughters unto glory.

Again, He came into the world to bear witness unto the truth. Again, He came that men might have life, that strange thing of which some are now asking whether it is "worth living." He came, and He knew, and had a great joy in knowing it, that they might have life, and that they might have it more abundantly.

These were some of His aspirations, some of His high aims. "Be of good cheer, I have overcome the world": that great saying summed up all His aspirations, and it was spoken—when ? Just a few hours before He went to His agony and to His cross.

My young friends, neither you nor I can measure the height of our Master's aspirations, but I know the very youngest of you can follow me when I say to you here to-day, at this your great school gathering : "Aspire, aim high, and as Christ's servant, not your own. Do not think of the prizes to be gained in that service ; the service is the prize."

The day before yesterday I was speaking to boys at a school nearly as old as your own, on their three hundredth birthday. Their school motto, surely a proud one, was this : "Suffer and serve." But you can look nearer home. What is the famous motto of the great Prince whose monument is the most stirring even of the many stirring monuments in this glorious Cathedral ? *I serve.* I am born not for myself, or for my parents, or for distinction, but for service—service to God, service to men. My education here as a boy is a failure unless it inspires and fosters—and how far sadder a failure if in any degree it quenches and stifles—this generous aspiration to serve. My life as a man will be a failure if I have not served; if no good cause for which brave men and high-minded women are struggling owns me as an ally; if, when the earthly end comes, I have broken no human yoke; if I have befriended no chivalrous enterprise; if I have thrown in my lot always with the comfortable and the prosperous who need little but congratulation, and seldom or never with the poor and the troubled who so sorely need service.

My young friends, I bid you, in the name of Jesus Christ, Aspire—aspire to serve. Resolve here at school that you will live no common, tame, self-indulgent lives, but "laborious days," with an eye fixed on a goal marked out by Christ Himself.

There is a well-known story of a group of illustrious friends meeting as very young men in a foreign university. One of them writes: "A spirit of zealous but friendly emulation arose amongst us; and on a certain cheerful evening, at my suggestion, we made a vow each to each other and to all that we would effect something great in our lives."*

Cynics may laugh in after life at such heroic

* See *Memoirs of Baron Bunsen*, 1868, vol. i. p. 46.

resolutions; boys will not; neither will they laugh who retain what is best in the boylike character, its generosity, its thirst for self-sacrifice, its contempt for the vulgar and commonplace, its belief that to youth and to labour and to daring, with the help of God, all things are possible.

Keep this conviction, my young friends, as one of the most precious parts of the inheritance of your boyhood. Abide in it, for in truth to abide in that is to "abide in Christ." To preserve unstained and "unspotted from the world" the ambition to serve your generation by the counsel of God, and, whether distinguished or obscure, to be "great in the sight of the Lord"—to do this, to keep this holy treasure of youth through all the changes and chances and disappointments of life is indeed "a hard thing." It will not come to you if you stand by yourself, unaided. You must have a strength not your own, and not anything that earth can give. Home, at its best, cannot give it; school, at its purest and bravest, cannot give it; public life and professional life cannot give it. You must abide in Christ, keep true to Him and in touch with Him, and, as He Himself says, feed on Him, eating His flesh and drinking His blood; taking your counsel from all you have gathered of His character; trying your plans and resolutions, even when they seem to be purest, by His all-perfect mind.

We have spoken of the individual soul abiding in Christ. Is there anything extravagant in extending the thought, and dreaming, if it be but for a moment, of a whole society abiding in Christ—a nation, a great national Church, a city, a school? Can you, boys of this school, lift your hearts to the conception of this historic school, its masters, its boys, its former members, all "abiding in Christ"; never leaving Him, never judging by any standard but His; counting here and through life as successes and distinctions only what He knows to be success and distinction; loving all truth as He loved it; sympathising, as He sympathised, with every human need and power and weakness; selecting from the vague mass of humanity each separate human soul as precious, and studying how to make it perfect; ministering with joy to every faculty of man, yet seeing every faculty as the gracious gift and the consecrated instrument of God?

My friends, if you do not see something of this vision in boyhood, you will never see it. Is it possible that on this day you do see something of it, and catch some slight reflexion of its splendour? If so, Christ, in whom you abide, has taken you with Him, if it be but for a moment, to the mount of His transfiguration and of yours; and, believe me, "it is good for us to be here."

"LORD, AND WHAT SHALL THIS MAN DO?"

RADLEY COLLEGE,
   Preached on June 29, 1889.

Peter seeing him saith to Jesus, Lord, and what shall this man do?—ST. JOHN xxi. 21.

"LORD, AND WHAT SHALL THIS MAN DO?"

IT is a question of reverent curiosity, one friend asking after the future of another friend. But what friends? Two men who have stamped themselves on the hearts and the souls of Christendom —the disciple who said, when the fortunes of his Master seemed almost at their lowest ebb, "Thou art the Christ, the Son of the living God," and the disciple to whom his Master, as He hung upon His cross, gave that one dying charge, "Behold thy Mother."

St. Peter's Day brings these two great Christians before us in the Second Lesson for the Morning Service. The scene is a touching one. Let us for a few moments look upon it. Peter had just passed through what perhaps we may call the last great crisis of his spiritual life. Doubtless other revelations were to be granted him. He was still to learn, in spite of early prejudices, that, in the new kingdom, "God was no respecter of persons, but that in every nation, he that feareth Him, and worketh righteousness, is accepted with Him." And again, he was still to show a momentary—it may be a more than momentary—forgetfulness of this great truth, and so to expose himself at Antioch to the censure of his brother Apostle, not indeed holier but even more enlightened than himself.

But these ebbs and flows of the tide of knowledge left, we must feel, the rock wholly unmoved. From the day that his loving Master put to him the threefold question, " Lovest thou me more than these love me ? " " Lovest thou me ? " " Lovest thou me ? " followed by the threefold charge, " Feed my lambs," " Shepherd my sheep," " Feed my sheep "—from that day, from that hour, the soul's anchorage of the fervent Apostle was safe. What could separate him from the forgiving love of Christ ? Faintheartedness in one miserable hour had done its worst. The snare was broken and he was delivered.

And now observe. Jesus Christ did not only forgive him his past frailty, He spoke also of his future destiny. Few things touch us so closely as

"LORD, AND WHAT SHALL THIS MAN DO?"

some "prophecy" that seems to "go before upon" any one that we love, some sign that seems to say, He is this to-day. He will become this to-morrow, and in years that we shall never see. Other fates are already linked with his. Now that he is young, we see promise and power; but "when he shall be old," already something of the veil is withdrawn.

Is there anything unreal in such language? Surely not, in a place like this, consecrated to youth. A great school is—must be—haunted by the spirit of prophecy.

But oh! think reverently what it must have been to an Apostle of Christ, a restored and forgiven and recommissioned Apostle, to hear from the lips of his Lord Himself words pointing to the coming years in which he should prove his untarnished loyalty: "Verily, verily, I say unto thee, when thou wast young thou girdedst thyself, and walkedst whither thou wouldest; but when thou shalt be old, thou shalt stretch forth thine hands, and another shall gird thee, and carry thee whither thou wouldest not. Now this He spake, signifying by what death he should glorify God."

In the past there had been youth, and all that

goes with youth—strength, independence, self-sufficiency, freedom, choice of career. Henceforward, the reverse; the career chosen for him by a mightier; the service, the suffering, the weakness, the helplessness, the outstretched arms finding no support, the painful, the inevitable death; and yet this death not the penalty but the crown of all, the death by which he should "glorify God." And when He had spoken this, when He had nerved His humbled but yet heroic soldier by the prospect of certain death in His service, then, knowing that He held him for ever, never more to flinch or desert, the great Master renewed to him the call of former days, the call which had first come to him amid the boats and the nets of the same Lake of Galilee, "Follow thou me."

This, my young friends, is part of the picture, but there is yet more. Perhaps we are never so unselfish and so loving as when we have been greatly moved by an overpowering joy or sorrow. We cannot think of ourselves alone. Other souls, other lives, other destinies press upon us, almost as part of ourselves. So here with St. Peter, while the old words "Follow me" were still ringing in his ears with their new and imperishable meaning,

"LORD, AND WHAT SHALL THIS MAN DO?"

"Peter, turning about, seeth the disciple whom Jesus loved following, who also leaned on His breast at the supper, and said, Lord, who is he that betrayeth Thee? Peter therefore seeing him saith to Jesus, Lord, and what shall this man do?"

These are the words that I chose for our text. I called them words of "reverent curiosity." The older man had heard something of his own future. Suffering, helplessness, death were before him. This was his "Prospice," and the prospect had put strength into his heart. What might not be in store for that younger life over which already so much of blessing seemed to hang? The impetuous Son of Thunder whom the gentlest of Masters seemed specially to love? The young zealot of whom the rest of the twelve had but lately been so jealous; who had asked, with his brother, to sit on the right hand and the left hand of Jesus in the new kingdom; who had said, "We saw one casting out devils in Thy name, and we forbade him, because he followed not with us"; and yet again, in the humble village of Samaria, "Lord, wilt Thou that we bid fire to come down from heaven and consume them?"

It was of this young man, this comrade of at

least three years, this witness with himself of so many sacred privacies, this eager, daring, yet profound and thoughtful spirit, who had been, it may be, an enigma to his fellows, it was of *him* that his elder friend now asked, " Lord, and what shall this man do ? " Is he, too, to be made perfect through suffering ? Will the day come, even for him, that he shall exchange the freedom of youth for the helplessness of age ? Will he, too, stretch out his hands and another gird him, and dare to carry that loved friend of ours and of Thine anywhere whither he would not ?

The question, whatever it may have meant, was, as you know, not fully answered. It was even gently, very gently, rebuked. If curiosity for others, if keen interest in the career of friends, leads us in the slightest degree to leave the path of our own clearly-marked devotion, we are, like Peter himself at Antioch, " to be blamed," and we need the reminder, however gentle, " Seekest thou great things for thy friend ? What is that to thee ? Follow thou me."

And yet we feel—the very genius of this place on this bright day of hope and onlook assures us—that there is a sense in which we may blamelessly and without danger ask for

"LORD, AND WHAT SHALL THIS MAN DO?"

one and another that is dear to us, "Lord, and what shall this man do?" Parents ask it for their sons. Masters ask it for their pupils. *You* ask it for your friends at school, and perhaps never more than at this time of the year, when, for not a few of you, the season of school life will so soon have passed for ever, and those who have been like brothers here will "part for manhood's race." Indeed, you cannot help such questioning. Curiosity is not only curiosity; it is also a teacher, or at least an impulse. It is to students of character what wonder is to students of Nature. If we might not look forward, if, in the strength of glorious self-effacement—so dear to every true teacher, "he must increase, but I must decrease"—we might not peer and even pry into the future for our children, our pupils, our friends—how poor, how narrow would be our dealings with them! It is impossible to be content with the "What is he now?" We must, perforce, just in proportion to the loving interest which he inspires, we must go on into the hereafter, with the question in any case, "What will he do?" and, if we are Christians, with the more sacred question, "Lord, who hast made him and lovest him, Lord, what shall this man do?"

It is a thought which has many uses. For one, it cheers us amid seeming failure. There are times—every educator knows them, every observer of young life knows them—when we seem at the end of our resources. We can make nothing of some strange character. It is either too strong for us, or too weak. Either it hates discipline just because it is discipline; it revolts and rebels. Or, again, it is too weak for any discipline to hold it upright; at all events, any discipline so free and trustful as that of a public school. It has no backbone. It needs propping, first on one side and then on another; and, in spite of all such assistance, it falls in the moral mire not once nor twice.

"Lord, and what shall this man do?" What is the Christian outlook for these characters that baffle us here, the almost desperately unruly, and the almost desperately weak?

Better often than we think or dare to hope.

Life does not end with school. In some natures it has hardly begun. Call them exceptional if you like, but at least recognise that they exist. And if they exist, there is One who cares for them and foresees what each "will do." School life, with its discipline adapted to the majority, cannot meet their needs. They must go elsewhere, and receive special training, each his own. If you trace them after they leave you, you will be met by strange surprises. Should war visit your country, the names of some of them will not be absent from forlorn hopes and desperate ventures.

Stranger still, some of them may hereafter be found on the Mission-field of the Church. One such case occurs to me as I write. Barely a year has passed since from, perhaps, the most dangerous of all dangerous parts of the wide Mission-field, truly carrying his life in his hand, an old pupil of mine, a school failure, wrote to confess some boyish offence which now—now that he was carried whither he would not, and seemed likely to be about to glorify God by his death—pressed upon his conscience, and craved even man's forgiveness. " Lord, and what shall this man do?" But a few years ago we should have answered the question gloomily. Now the Master of us all has taken into His own hands the young scholar with whom we failed, and has made of him a " vessel of choice," to bear His name among the heathen.

But it is not of seeming failure that we chiefly think when of one and another youthful friend or pupil we find ourselves saying, either in playful moments, "What will become of him?" or, in more thoughtful moments, "Lord, and what shall this man do?" Still more do we put this question of affectionate curiosity in cases of seeming promise.

What will he do, whom we have watched for four or five or six years, growing visibly in all that is best and fairest—the intellect gathering subtlety and force, the soul, so far as our eye can pierce, advancing from strength to strength? "Lord, and what shall this man do?"

Will he retain in the din and dust of life the straightforwardness and the chivalry which so far have been his charm? Will he become one of Christ's elect, a spiritual pillar of the Church or the nation, a trusted counsellor to high and low, the helper of noble causes while they are still feeble, willing to bear the Cross and despise the shame of many a brave but discredited venture of faith? Is it this that this man will do?

Or is he smaller, commoner than we suppose? Will flattery, or party, or sheer routine make conquest of him? Will he in some way "do well unto himself," and so bring no fruit to perfection even when it seemed so sure?

"LORD, AND WHAT SHALL THIS MAN DO?"

We do not answer the question; yet as each man or boy reverently, eagerly, almost breathlessly puts it of some present hero of his heart, we do not dare to check him with, "What is that to thee?" No, we recognise that, in putting so unselfish a question, he is standing on lofty and almost on holy ground. While striving to peer into the destinies of his friend, he is humbly re-laying the foundations of his own spiritual life.

Or, to take another case that we know so well at school, another case of high promise. This friend who has so long been a leader, foremost in all manly games, popular without effort, forced almost against his will to be influential, what will he do in the stress of life? That vigorous body, those buoyant spirits, that genial manner which at school secure so easy an ascendency—what will they be doing, what will they have done, twenty, thirty, forty years on? Will he still be somewhere at the front, a favourite among his fellows, a man whose smile and greeting are valued, whose word and will count for something in the contests of life?

It may be so; doubtless it often is so; but oh, how often do we, who have watched the life of schools, see exemplified in living flesh and blood the truth of the old words, "The last shall be first and the first last"!

A few years ago there were not many better judges of manliness, whether physical or moral, than John Lawrence of the Punjab, of whom it was said that "he feared man so little because he feared God so much." Soon after he returned from the Viceroyalty of India he said to me in substance, I do not remember the exact words, "How is it that your great athletes do not do more in after life? I have not come across them much." His experience, though wide, was that of but one man; yet, even taken alone, it is worth thinking over.

But prophecies of coming worth are not always falsified by events. More than three hundred years ago, in the household of Cardinal Morton, was brought up a young boy — devout, witty, insatiable for knowledge, irresistibly attractive — of whom that grey-haired statesman used to say, "Whoever may live to see it, this boy now waiting at table will turn out a marvellous man." That boy was the great Sir Thomas More, destined when young to walk whither he

"LORD, AND WHAT SHALL THIS MAN DO?"

would through every blameless path of the New Learning with his friends Erasmus and Colet, till he became Lord High Chancellor of England, but destined also, when he became old, to stretch forth his hands over the block of the executioner, and by a death of unsurpassed beauty to glorify God.

Will you bear, my young friends, with yet one other anecdote?

In one of our colleges at Cambridge is preserved the letter in which the most renowned orator and statesman of his age entrusted his son for the first time to the college tutor. The son was then but fourteen. "He is," says his father, "of a tender age, and of a health not yet firm enough to be indulged to the full in the strong desire he has to acquire useful knowledge... Such as he is, I am happy to place him at Pembroke, and I need not say how much of his parents' hearts goes along with him."

In these words the great Lord Chatham sent for the first time from home the young William Pitt. That delicate boy of fourteen, who joined the University younger than most of you now at school, was destined at twenty-one to enter the

House of Commons, and to die on the very same day exactly twenty-five years later, having been for nineteen of those years the most powerful Prime Minister that England has ever seen.

I have detained you too long. Yet there is a word that must be spoken, and spoken from the heart.

You, my friends, young and old, have the privilege and the pride of being members of an institution the very object of which is to create prophecies respecting youth, and to contribute by your training to their happy fulfilment. You are, even in a special sense, a Christian school. You are a nursery of the great Church of England. You live to strengthen her foundations, to put fresh blood into her veins, to renew her youth, to extend the arms of her world-wide beneficence. If you could foresee the future of your scholars, and if that future disclosed greatness, you would not be content if the greatness were only the greatness of the world. The woolsack of More and the premiership of Pitt are not the prizes that you have been taught to regard as the highest. It is your prayer that those who leave you may

"LORD, AND WHAT SHALL THIS MAN DO?"

become "great in the sight of the Lord"; may carry with them the true "pastoral" heart, the heart of the lay as well as of the clerical shepherd, who sees everywhere in Christ's redeemed world "lambs" to be "fed" and "sheep" to be "tended" in the great Shepherd's name.

With this object you have lived and worked and prayed and worshipped for more than forty years. Good men have watched over you, and given you their hearts and their very souls. And as it has been, so all promises to continue. You were never more full of hope and life than you are to-day. Boys of a former generation have become men. Boys of to-day, whose future is inexpressibly dear to you, are even now going forth to be men. Suffer a stranger, who knows the blessedness of such a life as yours, and whose heart is with you, to leave with you this morning, as a thought not unworthy of your bright and beautiful services and your happy gathering of friends, just this one question of a reverent and a truly Christian curiosity: "Lord, and what shall this man do?"

And may each young boy who hears the question, and imagines it as asked concerning himself, hear also a voice which, if obeyed, must make the answer a blessed certainty, "Follow thou me."

> Lord, and what shall this man do?
>   Ask'st thou, Christian, for thy friend?
> If his love for Christ be true,
>   Christ hath told thee of his end;
> This is he whom God approves,
> This is he whom Jesus loves.*

* Keble's *Christian Year*, St. John's Day.

SONS OF THE HIGHEST

WINCHESTER COLLEGE,
Preached in the Cathedral, July 12, 1891.

Ye shall be sons of the Highest.
ST. LUKE vi. 35.

SONS OF THE HIGHEST

"YE are the salt of the earth." "Ye are the light of the world." "Let your light shine before men, that they may see your good works." "Ye shall be sons of the Highest." These are some of the sayings of the Sermon on the Mount, from which our evening Lessons are just now taken, covering, in fact, six evenings of this month of July, from the 10th to the 15th.

They are very startling sayings. To whom were they spoken? Was it to great saints; to faithful martyrs; to learned defenders of the faith; to aged men who had walked with Christ for long years, and become models of all that gives dignity and grandeur to man? Not so. Just the contrary. Jesus is speaking to "His disciples," and that almost at the beginning of their discipleship. They are a few poor obscure men. They have just joined Him. They hardly know who He is. They have no notion what He will do for them and do with them, only they have found in Him something which they have found in no other. Call it a grace, or a charm, or an authority, or a spell, or what men now call a magnetism, there is something in Him which forces them to join Him. And He, in return, educates them and tells them what He expects from them. It is something new and different from the old. "It was said to them of old time"—what? Something formal, rigid, obvious; some act, or feeling, prompted by instinct and hardly condemned by reason: "An eye for an eye, and a tooth for a tooth"; "thou shalt love thy neighbour and hate thine enemy." "But I say unto you"—what? Some new thing, something deeper than act or even feeling, a new instinct, a new passion, a new creation: "Love your enemies"; "resist not evil"; "be ye perfect." And then, as one after another He gives these new and hard commands, He adds strange and startling words, like those with which I began: "Ye are the salt of the earth"; "ye are the light of the world"; "ye shall be sons of the Highest."

Now, of one thing at least we may be certain, Jesus Christ never flatters. If He astonishes His

SONS OF THE HIGHEST

disciples by telling them how great they are, it is not to make them vain and self-complacent. Before He has done with them, before their time of discipleship in His school has ended, He will again and again have shown them their dulness and their littleness.

But in these early days He wishes to lift them. They are not to be satisfied with the common. They are to be examples and witnesses and far-shining beacons. They are to remember their proud lineage. Not man but God is their Father. They are the "children," not of the world, nor of the earthly home, nor of the received tradition, but of the "Highest."

Now, I put it to you, my young friends, have we a right to apply such language to you? May we in all soberness and truth say to you, in this noble Cathedral which makes a part of the rich heritage of your boyhood, "Ye are sons of the Highest?" It is not likely that I shall ever speak to you again. I must therefore desire this evening to say something true and real which may dwell in your hearts and help you to live and die as Christian men. It is in this hope that I would try to put before you a thought with which you must indeed be familiar, and yet perhaps can never be weary of it. I mean your high privileges as members of this school. You belong to the very oldest of the great schools of England. You belong to it, and it, in a true sense, belongs to you. It is for a time your possession.

We know, indeed, that there may be greatness without antiquity. Youth may be great no less than age. Achilles, Pindar tells us, when a mere child, "played at mighty deeds." The child was father of the hero.

It is my good fortune to move much among the schools of England, and just as it gives me true delight to see the old schools renewing their youth and putting forth fresh leaves and fresh fruit with unexhausted and, please God, inexhaustible fertility, so also I rejoice at the splendid growth of the younger schools. Many of them have been founded or restored under my own eyes by dear friends of my own, and it does one's heart good to see them even now fashioning for themselves traditions of greatness, and learning to be proud of a life which they have rather created than inherited. If any of us were so foolish as to grudge them their prosperity, or imagine in our pride that no school could claim the name of "great" save after long years of past labour and triumph, we should be making just the same mistake that was made by an ancient people nearly nineteen hundred years ago, and we should need, in spirit if not in letter, precisely the same rebuke : "Think not to say within yourselves, We have Abraham to our father : for I say unto you, that God is able of these stones to raise up children unto Abraham."

Yes, God is able to take of the very humblest and apparently the most prosaic elements, and to raise up out of them mighty institutions—mighty empires, nations, armies, churches, colleges, schools. Nay, I doubt not that at this moment, if we had but the eyes to discern them, somewhere, in some obscure parts of our country, there are being laid deep the foundations of great intellectual and religious societies which in years to come may be linked for ever with illustrious names, and be the homes of an affection as deep and romantic as that which your own Winchester has for long centuries inspired in her children.

If, then, pride were our danger, we have perhaps said enough to humble. But let us turn now, without misgiving, to that innocent and noble form of pride, the pride which in every generation has been the strength of great nations, great

Churches, great educational institutions; the pride which breathes through that majestic Psalm which was chanted but three evenings back within these walls, and seems almost to claim this place—city, college, and cathedral—for its own : " Walk about Sion, and go round about her, and tell the towers thereof. Mark well her bulwarks, set up her houses, that ye may tell them that come after. For this God is our God for ever and ever; He shall be our guide unto death."

What, then, my young friends, is the lesson for you of your unequalled antiquity ? What is the value of your five hundred years in the sight, ay, and in the very house, of Him in whose sight a thousand years are but as yesterday ? You know the grand old motto of the French aristocracy, *Noblesse oblige.* High birth has its duties. For some centuries many of those nobles remained faithful to this generous ideal, and their country reaped the fruits. If history has on the whole recorded the stern verdict that a hundred years ago they almost deserved their unparalleled fall, it is because they came in time to forget the only truth which can justify privilege. They remembered that birth had its pleasures and its precedence and its Court glitter and its social ascendency.

They forgot, what their fathers and mothers had in better days remembered, that it had far more its duties and its responsibilities.

And so it is with great and ancient Schools. If their antiquity begets a devoted and self-forgetting love; if it inspires a thankfulness and a pride, seldom spoken of, seldom pointed to, but always there and always burning; if it brings to mind the simplicity, the piety, the manliness, ay, and even the rough hardships of other days; if it summons before the imagination great and good men in almost every department of public life, and whispers, even in careless ears, that this place was as dear to them a hundred, two hundred, three hundred, four hundred, five hundred years ago as it is to you to-day; if, further, it suggests some such thought as this: "God, who is no respecter of persons, cannot have kept watch over us for so many centuries, 'from one generation to another,' without purposing that we should offer to Him and to His people some more than common service"—then, my friends, your antiquity is not a snare to you but a power. It intertwines itself with every grateful retrospect and every chivalrous aspiration. It makes part both of the life which you now breathe and of the career that lies before you. "You are sons of the Highest," even in the ranks of earthly lineage, but how much more in the ranks of a spiritual descent!

For your antiquity has never been a pagan antiquity. You were dedicated to God in your earliest infancy five hundred years ago, and there has been a continuity of dedication all your days. You have never been paganized and never re-baptized. The cathedral and the chapel have never been mere adjuncts and excrescences of your life. They have always been a part of it. Nay, our presence here this summer evening is in itself a proof that the old tradition is still alive. When we speak of the blessing of an ordered life of Christian discipline, of direct Christian influences, of regular hours of Christian worship and of Christian prayer, we are not pointing to an ideal of the future, but simply reminding you of your own past. "I write no new commandment unto you." I have not that presumption. I do but quote to you the well-known words of one of your own saintliest sons: "O Philotheus, you cannot enough thank God for the order of the place you live in, where there is so much care taken to make you a good Christian, as well as a good scholar ; where you go frequently to prayers every day in the chapel and in the school, so that you are in a manner brought up in a perpetuity of prayer."

These words of Ken have been "household words" to Wykehamists for more than two hundred years. But even when they were written, there were three hundred years of school life behind them. He was not dreaming dreams, but seeing actual visions. He was even then appealing with thankfulness to the past. Surely, then, there are no living scholars to whom one may more fitly say in the days of their youth, "You cannot enough thank God for the order of the place you live in." You that "are in a manner brought up in a perpetuity of prayer" may find it easier than some others to believe that you are indeed "sons of the Highest," not only the "children of your generation," nor the children of society, nor even the children of your venerable college, but yet more than this, the children of the Highest, the children of Him who heareth prayer, and *is* in Himself all greatest and holiest ideals.

My friends, I can imagine the more thoughtful among you saying to themselves—I can imagine masters, fresh perhaps from the Universities where life is less simple, saying to themselves—"Yes, this is an ideal: this is vague, shadowy, mere words and sentiment, suited perhaps to an exceptional mood on an exceptional day, but not made for the wear and tear of week days, for the happy *abandon* of the cricket-ground, for the petty temptations of the study and the schoolroom."

Yes, sermons need touchstones; and these, no doubt, are the touchstones to apply to them. Even the Sermon on the Mount, with its long roll of almost desperate ideals, must, we reverently feel, have done little good to those who heard it unless it strengthened them day by day, during the remainder of their lives, for the "trivial round" and "the common task."

It is not ideals that make us conquerors. "He that overcometh," he that, after the long struggle, is to "stand before the Son of Man," humbled, self-emptied, purified by discipline, made perfect by suffering, must have fed on a spiritual food more solid and more divine than the ideals which our own hearts have created. Still we know that, in God's hands, an ideal set up in boyhood does often prove the very angel and guide of a career.

To be "a son of the Highest," what is it for a

boy at school? I can only tell you a little, but it is at least this—to say to oneself every day, and, in saying it to oneself, to say it to God : "I am Thine. Keep me at Thy level. Keep me from all that lowers, all that is untrue, unclean, unkind, ungenerous, unloving. When the low thing is put before me, as a bait, or a lure, or a prize, or an ambition, show me the Highest, show me Thyself. Remind me that there, with Thee, not here, with this lower thing, is my birth and my home. If ever the wings of conscience grow weary, if ever I am tempted to accept the average, to acquiesce in the commonplace, to admit that some sins are necessary and some temptations irresistible; if ever I say to myself, or all but say it, ' I will be as others, no worse, no better ; I will be like the other nations, and have, like them, an average king of my soul'—then, O Eternal Father of youth and weakness, admonish me of my high calling in Christ Jesus. Come to me in that moment of dimness and frailty, and help me to 'lift up my heart,' as in happier hours, to believe that I am one of the 'sons of the Highest,' and that the high God is my Redeemer."

Is this ideal too high for the youngest here? No, I believe that it will be easier for them to accept it as natural and obvious than for some of those to whom they seem so childish. "Do but consider how welcome a young convert is to God," is another of the sayings of the holy Ken, so impressive by its very audacity, as though it asked us to put ourselves in the place of the great Father, and sympathise with Him in His joy at winning a young soul. It is not the young soul which will most be startled by this holy audacity. To them, I repeat, the call seems natural and obvious, and the reason is because the words of Christ state a fact and not only an ideal. We *are* sons of the Highest. We *are* partakers of the divine nature. Ah! if we can but grow up with this certainty as one of our school traditions, one of the convictions which make men of us, growing with our growth and strengthening with our strength, how much of those sad arguments which others need is, thank God, unneeded by us.

For instance, in the Epistle for to-day, St. Paul has to argue with his spiritual children. He asks them: "What fruit had ye then in those things whereof ye are now ashamed? For the end of those things is death." And in like manner the good Ken, if I may quote him once more, puts much the same sad question to his young Win-

SONS OF THE HIGHEST

chester pupil: "O Philotheus, do but ask any one old penitent, what fruit, what satisfaction he hath purchased to himself by all those pleasures of sin which flattered him in his youth, and of which he is now ashamed. Will he not sadly tell you he has found them all to be but vanity and vexation of spirit?"

Indeed, there is but one answer to such a question. All life, the life of good men and of bad men, the life of pagan alike and Christian, is a lie, and all its experience is a lie, if the end of these things, these indulgences of the lower nature, is not indeed death.

But, O brethren, let us by God's great mercy so live in these happy days of our youth, so use and so be thankful for "the order of this place we live in," that such an argument, necessary for some, may have no terrors, nay, hardly a meaning, for us. We are sons of the Highest. Let us live ever with our Father, for all that He has is ours.

I have quoted to you the argument of one great Apostle. I will leave with you, as my latest message, the glorious appeal of another. St. John knew what life was, and what the world was, and what sin was. He wrote, so he tells us, to his little children because they had known the Father. He wrote, he tells us, to young men because they were strong, not weak and effeminate and cowardly, but because they were strong, and the word of God abode in them, and they had already overcome the wicked one. And then, to beloved human souls, so trained, so endowed, so rich in their glorious ideals and their splendid environment, he says, in language as practical as it is sublime : " Beloved, now are we the sons of God, and it hath not yet been made manifest what we shall be. We know that if He be made manifest we shall be like Him, for we shall see Him as He is. And every man that hath this hope in Him," ay, every man or boy who knows in his heart, and exults to know it, that he is one of the sons of the Highest, " purifieth himself even as He is pure."

"STAND FAST IN THE FAITH, QUIT YOU LIKE MEN"

WELLINGTON COLLEGE,
Preached on June 19, 1892, the day after the annual Speech Day.

Stand fast in the faith, quit you like men.
1 COR. xvi. 13.

"STAND FAST IN THE FAITH, QUIT YOU LIKE MEN"

ONE of the best known stories of the great battle of which we were all thinking yesterday is this : One regiment was hard pressed, and suffering seriously from the enemy's fire. Presently Wellington rode up and called out : " Stand firm, Ninety-fifth ! We must not be beaten. What would they say in England ? " Stand firm ! It was an appeal to the manliness of his soldiers, and to their patriotism. The eye of their country was upon them. Whether charged by the cavalry or mowed down by the cannon, there must be no flinching. Stand firm ! We must not be beaten !

My young friends, any stranger who speaks to you from this pulpit can hardly avoid thoughts and figures of a warlike colour. On any day it would be difficult to avoid them. After an anniversary like that of yesterday it becomes, at all events for me, impossible. Other schools have their yearly festival on days which are either in themselves convenient, or recall some personal memory whether in the State or the Church. For example, your neighbours at Eton have their "Fourth of June." It is the birthday of King George the Third, who had a great affection for their famous school, so close to his own castle-palace.

Another flourishing school,* not very far distant, has chosen St. Peter's Day, the 29th of June. I have spoken to the boys there myself on that day from their chapel pulpit. But you, my friends, have chosen for your yearly festival—chosen it by a happy necessity, which other schools might envy—the memory of a great battle, one might call it an ideal battle, because, as Wellington himself finely said, "Waterloo did more than any battle I know of towards the true object of battles—the peace of the world."

This great battle, with all its heroism and all its sacrifices, is for you even more than what it is, or ought to be, for all true Englishmen. To them it should be for all time a matter of devout thankfulness to the Giver of all national blessings: "We

* Radley College.

"STAND FAST IN THE FAITH"

have heard with our ears, O God, our fathers have told us, what things Thou hast done in their time of old."

But to you it means the very "reason of your being." It might almost be said that you were born at Waterloo. Your name, your motto, your relics, your memorials, your anniversary, all carry back the mind to one heroic figure and one immortal struggle. Custom, I suppose, must, with some of you, as with too many of us who dwell in the holy places of history, or of learning, have dulled to some extent the proper daily inspiration of these ancestral memories, but to a stranger all is still astir. To a stranger who is privileged to visit you in your own home—shall I say restored to your own home after a brief but memorable migration?—all that he sees on the 18th of June speaks of Wellington and of Waterloo.

And therefore when, on the morning that follows it, one tries to offer you words of Christian counsel, one's thoughts almost perforce turn to one side of the Christian life—I mean the life of the Christian militant, the life of the good soldier of his King and Leader, the life which tests Christian manliness, and is so nobly summed up in the two trumpet words of the great Apostle:

Στήκετε, ἀνδρίζεσθε — *Stand fast. Quit you like men.*

Manliness has, of course, many sides and many graces, but on this day and in this place I shall speak of only one. The men who died at Waterloo, as it were yesterday, would pardon me if I singled out for the reverence of their young countrymen their unflinching courage. In their name, I would say to you, "Learn Christian manliness by being courageous." Easy to say, hard to do. School life brings with it many blessings not equally to be found at home, but it brings also—you know it as well as I—some special dangers. Home often tempts you to be selfish and lazy and ill-tempered, but it does not often tempt you to be cowardly. But school does at times tempt you to be cowardly. You dare not say what you really feel. You see certain acts done, you hear certain words spoken, which utterly revolt you. They offend your taste alike and your conscience. They are at once coarse and wicked. If you were your natural self, if you were at home and heard them mentioned as being the fashion at some other place, you would despise and detest the fashion. You would speak out at once, and show your scorn. But now, with just a few companions

"STAND FAST IN THE FAITH"

standing round, you dare not. For your life you dare not. All the soldier, all the man, has gone out of you, and when the soldier and the man are gone, the Christian is gone too. It is at these moments that the enemy is upon you. Oh for some voice to whisper, or, if need be, thunder in our ears, "*Stand fast. Quit you like men!*" Act as brave men act in battle. They dare not there be cowards. They cannot, they must not, be beaten. What will they say in England? A greater eye is upon them—a grander, a holier presence. That presence, once felt, reawakens all that makes courage easy—the spell of discipline, the charm of comradeship, the thrill of loyalty to a leader, the sacred pride of devotion to a cause.

"Which things are an allegory." The youngest of you can, I think, read its meaning. You can see who the Leader is whom the Christian soldier follows, and what is the august fatherland of those who, with earth's best blessings in their grasp, yet "desire a better country, that is, a heavenly."

To love the very name of this country, to be jealous of its honour, to fight as it were under its flag—nor ever suffer that flag to be lowered, much less lost—this is the proud ambition of the Christian, and this ambition is manliness.

We have on the walls of our chapel at Harrow—a chapel built by the same architect and almost at the same time as your own—a small marble tablet in memory of two young officers,* one trained at Harrow, the other at Haileybury—who between them saved the colours at the disastrous fight at Isandlana in South Africa, but in saving them met their deaths. Upon this tablet we engraved three lines, which were written at the time by one of the oldest and one of the most illustrious Englishmen then living, I mean Lord Stratford de Redcliffe, the famous Ambassador at Constantinople during the Crimean War. He wrote them when he was about ninety-three years old, just after he heard of the heroic deaths of the two young men :

Ye crown the list of glorious acts which form our country's boast ;
Ye rescued from the brink of shame what soldiers prize the most ;
And reached, by Duty's path, a life beyond the lives ye lost.

Touching tribute from old age to true soldierly courage in the young ! It was their manliness that came home to the old statesman and won his praise, and in so praising them he was but giving utterance to the admiring gratitude of the whole nation.

* Lieutenant Teignmouth Melvill and Lieutenant Coghill.

"STAND FAST IN THE FAITH"

With you, my young friends, at school the opportunity for Christian manliness is, of course, outwardly different. There are no two armies pitched opposite each other, army against army, with a valley between them, as when David ran to meet Goliath. There is no beloved flag waving visibly over the head of each regiment. There is no Hougomont definitely entrusted to one brave officer,* to be held to the last. There is no sudden rush of brilliant horsemen, to be met again and again in square with timely and deadly volley.

Our warfare and our weapons are spiritual. Our battlefield, as seen by the outward eye, has little either to stimulate or to warn. Think how poor a thing it sometimes is—just a knot of bad, dull boys round a fire, among them not one whom any respect. They are laughing and talking after their kind, perhaps of things of which "it is a shame even to speak"; perhaps sneering at honest discipline, or study, or religious custom; perhaps laughing down some young boy's examples and high principle.

This is at times the battlefield of a young Christian soldier at school. How poor and

* Macdonnell.

vulgar it sounds beside the names of Waterloo or Salamanca or Vittoria! And yet it is a field on which wounds can be felt and palms can be won.

This was the kind of battlefield to which Arnold would so often refer, that great teacher to whom, after fifty years, a monument * is to be placed among the heroes of the nation. To him the great curse of Public Schools, to be set against their noble powers for good, the great curse seemed to be—I quote his brilliant pupil and biographer—"the spirit" sometimes "there encouraged of combination, of companionship, of excessive deference to the public opinion prevalent in the school." Once he spoke of it in these stern words—are they even now obsolete?—"If the spirit of Elijah were to stand in the midst of us, and we were to ask him, 'What shall we do then?' his answer would be, 'Fear not, nor heed one another's voices, but fear and heed the voice of God only.'" And the favourite image of human goodness which always stood out before Arnold was the noble portrait of Abdiel in Milton:

* A meeting with this object had been held at Westminster a few days before, on Monday, June 13.

"STAND FAST IN THE FAITH"

> The Seraph Abdiel, faithful found
> Among the faithless, faithful only he ;
> Among innumerable false, unmov'd,
> Unshaken, unseduc'd, unterrified,
> His loyalty he kept, his love, his zeal ;
> Nor number, nor example, with him wrought
> To swerve from truth, or change his constant mind,
> Though single.

It is to courage of this kind, this simple moral courage, that you, my friends, are called now in these happy days of your youth. The great Christian teacher of whom I have just spoken, and to whom every Christian school, this not the least, owes so deep a debt, when pleading for the courage of an Abdiel among boys at school, was but echoing the words of Christ's Apostle which we chose for our text. If I could hope that any word of mine might reach any young heart here this morning, I would say, "Stand fast in the faith. Quit you like men." Make it your special prayer to-day that God may increase in you this high gift of courage. Begin with it in small things, and begin at once. The very next time you see or hear anything bad, do not assent, or seem to assent. Show in some way that you can be yourself and stand alone. If tempted to say what is untrue, or not quite the truth, ask for courage. If ashamed, or half ashamed, at any time to pray, or to read the Bible, or to attend the Holy Communion, ask for courage. If you see any little boy unkindly treated, or tempted to go wrong, and some one is wanted to stand up for him, pray for courage to be his helper. These, you say, are all small matters. Yes, they are, and that is why I choose them. They are combats, not pitched battles, but it is in combats and skirmishes that the courage is learned which wins Waterloos.

Christian manliness is learned by being practised. It is learned little by little, just as cowardice is learned little by little. Christian manliness is learned by remembering God, and duty, and honour just at the moment when the trial comes. And the trial mostly " cometh not with observation." It steals upon us, like an enemy in the mist. There is no time for closing ranks and forming square. We must stand alone, and fight alone. That is Christian courage.

A school which can train boys in courage of this kind is training men for God and their country. You will find as you grow older that courage is a rare gift in public life. Few men think and act for themselves. Most men are on

"STAND FAST IN THE FAITH"

the watch for the loudest not the loftiest voices. They are so used to follow that they have lost the nerve to lead. To you I would point out the "more excellent way." In boyhood, as in manhood, "be strong and very courageous." Such was the charge given to Joshua, that brave and devout soldier, who is the hero of the three Lessons of this Sunday.*

Such was the life-teaching and the legacy of the great man whose name it is your proud privilege to bear. Such is the teaching of your great annual festival. Oh what a Sunday was that just seventy-seven years ago, when our countrymen and their allies, all, as it were, held together in the iron grasp of one man, "stood fast" during those long summer hours, and "quitted themselves like men!" How much of the blessings that we Englishmen now enjoy—nay, how almost all of the blessings that you Wellington boys now enjoy—is due to the courage then shown by them! How much they did as the soldiers of their country that we as the soldiers of Christ may pray to copy! I know, and you know, that He has other lessons to teach us of a yet higher order, and that the glory of the saint and the sufferer and the faithful

* The First Sunday after Trinity.

183

witness is yet purer and more majestic than the glory of the warrior. But courage is one of our Master's gifts. He expects it from all. He expects it from all, because He grants it to each, if they will but ask Him for it. It is to those who fight for Him that He is very gracious. He that stands fast and quits him like a man is "he that overcometh," ὁ νικῶν. For him He reserves some of His highest honours and most precious promises. Of "him that overcometh" glorious things like these are spoken :

"Him that overcometh will I make a pillar in the temple of my God, and he shall go no more out."

"He that overcometh, the same shall be clothed in white raiment, and I will confess his name before my Father and His angels."

"To him that overcometh will I grant to sit with me in my throne, even as I also overcame, and am set down with my Father in His throne."

"FEAR GOD: HONOUR THE KING"

WESTMINSTER SCHOOL,
    Preached in the Abbey on
Election Sunday, July 29, 1894.

Fear God : honour the king.
1 PETER ii. 17.

"FEAR GOD: HONOUR THE KING"

OUR Public Schools are favourites of the English people. They are watched with sympathy and regard. No one grudges them their fame. A public man, whether in Church or State, is liked all the better, and seems, if I may say so, something more of an Englishman, if he is known to be a son, and a loyal son, of one of our great schools.

I make no apology, Christian friends, for addressing myself this morning mainly to the boys of the famous school which alone has the privilege of worshipping in these venerable walls. A custom of, I suppose, some three centuries brings together, as on this day, every year the representatives of two of the greatest Colleges of Oxford and Cambridge, and the representatives of St. Peter's College, Westminster. The "three Royal Colleges," as they are called, meet in spirit, and wish one another prosperity. How is it possible for a man of Christian or of patriotic feeling to see this young life year after year passing before him without having his heart stirred with something warmer than official sympathy? If on this morning we can say a word in season to the Westminster boys, our elder friends will, I know, more than forgive us.

"Fear God: honour the king." True religion! Reverent patriotism! What a trumpet call to a great school! Add one thing more, intellectual enthusiasm, and you have pretty well summed up what a school should teach. With the last we do not deal to-day in this place, but the very anniversary which brings us here, uniting as it does in historic sisterhood three royal seats of learning, has surely a lay sermon of its own. It bears witness that this great school is pledged, by its very charter, to be the fostering nurse of intellectual enthusiasm and of the inborn faith of the mind of man in whatsoever things in literature or in science are true and beautiful and august.

But now to our special work. "Fear God: honour the king." Fear God. Can this indeed be taught and practised at a public school? More than a hundred years ago your own Christian

"FEAR GOD: HONOUR THE KING"

poet, William Cowper, would have said, "Impossible." In that scathing satire which he launched at public schools, and which feebler men have never ceased to quote, he was painting, as he thought, from the life. He was recalling old and unhappy memories of his own. Not that Cowper was not keenly alive to the charm of old school ties. Every public school-boy should know and love the famous lines:

> Be it a weakness, it deserves our praise,
> We love the play-place of our early days;
> The scene is touching, and the heart is stone
> That feels not at that sight, and feels at none.
> The wall on which we tried our graving skill,
> The very name we carved subsisting still,
> The bench on which we sat while deep employ'd,
> Though mangled, hacked, and hewed, not yet destroy'd.

But the man who felt all this and expressed it so delightfully was cold and dumb as to another class of memories. No religious memories were linked with Cowper's Westminster. Its friendships, its studies, its *esprit de corps*, had helped him to much, but they had not helped him to "fear God." Such teaching was reserved for later days.

Carry on your thoughts to a time, distant indeed to you, but near to the thoughts of many of us, the time of the Crimean War, that war which gave you your proud school monument just outside Dean's Yard. When the tidings of the first battles of that war reached England, another illustrious member of your school, the wise and holy Bishop Cotton, spoke in this way to the boys of another public school,* which has become in a peculiar manner allied with your own. "In war," he said, "and in peace, at school and at home, as a boy and as a man, each of you is warned to value duty even above life, and to remember that the only true way of knowing duty and doing his duty when danger and death are around him, is to preserve unbroken the tie which binds him to Jesus Christ his Lord."

Those last words would have seemed strange to Cowper in the days of his boyhood here. Nay, they would, I think, have seemed strange even to Cotton himself in the days of his boyhood just before he came up to us at Trinity sixty years ago. But to you, my young friends, the language does not sound strange. Thank God, your boyhood has fallen at a time when the service of Christ and even the love of Christ are a natural part of school thoughts, and when no education of boys in any

* Marlborough College.

"FEAR GOD: HONOUR THE KING"

rank of life is counted other than a failure unless it has taught them to " fear God."

And yet how hard it is even for the best among us to put a true meaning of his own into the almost too ready phrase, the " fear of God."

We know indeed that it means nothing servile, nothing cowardly, nay, that it is just the one thing which makes cowardice impossible. We have heard of the line of the French poet : * " I fear God, dear Abner, and have no other fear."

We have heard of that stout-hearted statesman over whose honoured grave you pass to and fro in coming to this choir—I mean, of course, John Lawrence of the Punjab—that "he feared man so little because he feared God so much." This "gospel of courage" has been again and again both sounded and fulfilled in your ears, till even the timid have come to believe that in the reverent fear of God is the one secret of shelter from the face of the enemy.

School, my friends, even the worst school, is a splendid training-place in the fear of God. Home, with its gentleness and its sympathies, and so much, as it were, "made easy" for virtue, has other and milder lessons of its own. But this

* Racine's *Athalie*.

fear of God, how mightily is it taught at school, sometimes in the first year, the first term, nay, the first day! To stand out when "fools make a mock of sin;" to refuse to smile or to join when the bad jest is made, or the bad trick proposed; to stand firm among laughing or menacing companions, "unshaken, unseduced, unterrified"—this is not seldom the prize of the battle of school life, and again and again, thank God, the prize is won. And if it is won, it is won not by good feeling only, or good taste, or good sense, or by a mere delicacy of sentiment which abhors whatever is coarse; no, a stronger and less earthly panoply than any of these is needed; it is the reverent fear of God."

More than thirty years ago a great Head Master,* to whom I owe much, and whose life during the last few months has been visibly precious to his countrymen, spoke thus to the boys of a beloved school which he had nobly served: "My brethren, there are many things which I desire for this place. I desire that it should be a home of diligence, of kindness, of knowledge, of happiness. I desire that it should be known as one in which good

---

* Dr. Vaughan, Dean of Llandaff, formerly Head Master of Harrow.

"FEAR GOD: HONOUR THE KING"

learning is successfully cultivated, and from which there go forth year by year those who shall serve their country in its different departments with success and honour. But I declare to you that at this time I would sacrifice all else, all worldly and all loftier aspirations in your behalf, for the single assurance that there was at work amongst you, in your lessons, in your games, in your houses, in your rooms, above all, in your hearts, a genuine fear of God, a sense of His presence, of His observation, of His law, of His judgment, a dread of displeasing Him in word or act."

He was right, this Christian teacher, who taught what Cowper would have believed to be unteachable. He taught what boys, no less than men, are eager and thankful to believe. The "fear of the Lord," in this noble sense, is the base of all religion, all religion that will last. The "fear of the Lord" is the beginning of wisdom. The "fear of the Lord" is safety. The "fear of the Lord" is watchfulness against danger. The "fear of the Lord" is unflinching courage when and in whatever form the danger comes.

We have heard one part of our school training. Let us now listen to another. "Fear God : honour the king." In St. Peter's mouth "the king" must have been the Roman Emperor. The man may have been utterly bad, but he was the symbol of lawful authority, and as such he was to be honoured. To us, in our day, the command " Honour the king " seems easy indeed; it is part of an Englishman's birthright. So it was when your school was founded by the great Queen Elizabeth; so it was two hundred and fifty years ago when your eloquent schoolfellow, Dr. South, bore this testimony to your forefathers : " Westminster is a school which neither disposes men to division in Church nor sedition in State; a school so untaintedly loyal that I can truly and knowingly aver that in the very worst of times in which it was my lot to be a member of it, we were really 'king's scholars' as well as called so. Nay, upon that very day, January 30th, that black and eternally infamous day of the King's murder, I myself heard, and am now a witness, that the King was publicly prayed for in this school, but an hour or two at most before his sacred head was struck off."

Loyalty to a person is easy. Loyalty to a principle is harder. That country is happy in which the person and the principle are so closely and so dearly knit together that the loyalty of conscience becomes also a loyalty of affection,

"FEAR GOD: HONOUR THE KING"

and has passed long since from a duty into an instinct and a passion. But the word of the Apostle knows nothing of political constitutions or of earthly frontiers. Its sound is gone out into all lands. In America, in Switzerland, in France, which as on this day sixty-four years ago hurled from his throne the last of the Bourbons, the same spiritual voice is still heard, "Honour the king." And to all alike it says, whether the subjects of a monarchy or the citizens of a republic, "Reverence authority. Hold rulers in respect for their work's sake. Love your country not as citizens only, or as gentlemen only, but as Christians." *In patriam populumque,* "For country and for people," is the proud motto of your school. Let it sink deep into your hearts as a voice not of man only but of God. Rejoice that during these happy years of boyhood you are training yourselves not only for knowledge or wealth or professional success, but also for the service of your country, some in the field, some in India, some in the Church, some in business, some in Parliament. Bring to this service of "country and people" a true reverence for government, a resolve to see in it something august and something divine, not a hubbub of random voices, or a pitiful conflict of clashing interests, but the growing sense of human brotherhood, and the conviction that each man, each class, each profession, each Church, each nation can take to itself no grander motto than the Christian's one social and political demand: *I serve.*

Happy the school that sends forth scholars so reverencing authority and so devoting themselves to their country! You, my friends, have sent forth many such. It is this way that your traditions point.

> Great men have been among you, hands that penned,
> And tongues that uttered wisdom.

Statesmen have been among your staple products. For them, *In patriam populumque* had at least a secular voice. For you, let its voice be not secular only but Christian. So interpreted, it calls you not more to reverence than to sympathy, and, in bidding you "honour the king," bids you also honour the "king's people," so indeed echoing the prayer of the Psalm, that majestic coronation hymn of all true government, "Give the king thy judgments, O God, and thy righteousness unto the king's

"FEAR GOD: HONOUR THE KING"

son. So shall he judge thy people according unto right, and defend the poor."

This it is, this natural union of reverence and of sympathy, which gives so much value to all those "Missions,"* whether of schools or of colleges, which have sprung up so swiftly in these later years. Yours, my young friends, is one of these. You ask for it to-day our sympathy and our help. You tell us that for both of these there is an urgent need. You ask every man and every woman here present to aid you in the discharge of a new school duty. *In patriam populumque*, your old motto, has found a fresh voice. Many an old Westminster statesman has lived for it in the past. Many an old Westminster soldier has died for it in battle. It now summons you to bloodless victories for the poor and the needy. In this good work I cannot but think and hope that many of us will be glad to stand by you to-day and become for the moment Westminster boys. Anyhow, I am sure that no man or woman can see you here to-day on the eve of your breaking-up, some of you to return no more as boys to this illustrious school, without wishing

* There was a collection on behalf of the Westminster School Mission.

you God-speed in the lives that lie before you. May they be lives deeply rooted in the "fear of God," and fruitful in service to this "kingly commonwealth of England!" At every stage of those lives, in quiet days when heroism slumbers, in stirring and perilous days which call for daring and for leadership, alike in every victory and in every defeat, may you keep untainted both your faith and your loyalty; may you "fear God and honour the king!"

THE RICH AND THE POOR

ETON COLLEGE,
Preached on July 21, 1895, for the
Eton Mission at Hackney Wick.

There were two men in one city; the one rich, and the other poor.—2 SAM. xii. 1.

THE RICH AND THE POOR

SO it was in the days of David at Jerusalem. So it was in the days of the Gracchi at Rome. So it was in the days of the French Revolution at Paris. So it is now in London. In the same city there are "two men," and two classes of men, "the one rich, and the other poor."

What do they know and think of each other? How do they act, how ought they to act, towards each other? One kind of answer is given by the world, another by the Church; one by our ordinary habits, another by our conscience when something has deeply stirred it.

Again, one kind of answer is given in Pall Mall by the luxurious Club, another at Hackney Wick by such a body as your Eton Mission.

That Mission of yours, my young friends, could answer many hard questions—not, indeed, that hardest of all, that old old question, Why it is that in every city there are always two classes of men, the smaller one rich and the vastly greater one poor, and whether this state of things is destined to last as long as our earth is the home of man.

But it can answer another question, far more pressing and for us far more fruitful. Given these two classes, existing side by side, can anything be done to make them know one another better and care for each other more? There are many of us who think that to answer this question wisely is just the main task of our time; that, as compared with it, most of the political questions which are now in the air, the too heated air, of controversy, such as changes in the Constitution, and alterations of the franchise, and disestablishment of Churches, and abolition of privileges, are mere cries—"a sounding brass or a tinkling cymbal." None of these changes, whether they be good or bad, will make the rich man love the poor more or the poor man love the rich more, and it is just this increase of love between rich and poor—real genuine love and mutual respect—which is the one hope of the future, the very bond of civilisation and of all social virtues.

THE RICH AND THE POOR

Now let us all, young and old, be as honest and simple as we can. Does any boy, any younger boy, say in his heart of hearts, "What have I to do with the poorer classes? I have never come in touch with them, I never entered their homes, I have never done them harm; but why am I called upon to do them good? They have their life, and I have mine. Why should we not go each our own way? Why should we cross each other's path?"

I will try to answer your question, my young friends, because I take for granted that you put it in all honesty, and not with anything of a wretched unmanly sneer. I will give you two reasons why you should care about the poor. Many more might be added, but two will be enough.

One shall be what you must permit me to call an Etonian reason; the other shall be a Christian reason.

The Etonian reason has a voice, no doubt, for others as well as for you, but it has a voice for you—you will be proud to admit it—even louder than for all others. It is this, my friends, that so much has been given to you; that, in the sight of God, you are so rich; that, in the words of the great parable which stirred the soul of David, you have such "exceeding many flocks and herds." Where, if not here, in what spot of England more than this—not certainly at Oxford or at Cambridge—could a man take this great word of the Prophet in his hand, and, looking his hearers straight in the face and insisting on the obligations of the rich and the fortunate, say finally to each of them one by one, "Thou art the man; it is thou to whom God has sent me"?

And now, mark me, wherever these obligations are joyfully appropriated, wherever the hearer looks up and answers, "Yes, it is I, and I am thankful for the reminder," there is in the air of that society greatness. Nay, there may be a touch even of the heroic. Do some of you remember that fine passage in Homer—one statesman,* at least, more than a century since, bore witness to its inspiring power—where the Lycian king, Sarpedon, proud of his high lineage and large possessions, urges his princely comrade to claim the foremost place in danger and in toil?

* Lord Granville, a few days before his death in 1762. The story is told in Matthew Arnold, *On Translating Homer*, 1861, pp. 16–18.

THE RICH AND THE POOR

> Why boast we, Glaucus, our extended reign,
> Where Xanthus' streams enrich the Lycian plain,
> Our numerous herds that range the fruitful field,
> And hills where vines their purple harvest yield?
> Why on those shores are we with joy survey'd,
> Admired as heroes, and as gods obey'd,
> Unless great acts superior merit prove,
> And vindicate the bounteous powers above?
> 'Tis ours, the dignity they give, to grace,
> The first in valour as the first in place.*

Yes, that last line appeals to every generous heart, whether in man or boy.

> The first in valour as the first in place.

Which of you would disown that claim? Which of you would renounce that obligation? You do not renounce it. You admit it. You would be indignant if any man strove to rob you of it. As Cabinet after Cabinet is captained by an Etonian chief; as the "first place" on both sides of both Houses is, Parliament after Parliament, filled by some Eton statesman; as the direction of foreign affairs, of the chief Embassies abroad, of India, of Canada, of the great Colonies on the other side of the globe is again and again entrusted to Etonian hands, you do recognise—some of you with pride,

* Pope's *Iliad*, xii. 374.

some with a gratitude which is greater than pride—that all this prominence has its responsibilities, and calls upon every Etonian in his profession, his regiment, his counting-house, his country parsonage, his bishopric at home or his bishopric in Australia, or New Zealand, or the islands of the Pacific, to bestir himself and come to the front, and risk his life and his substance for the country and the Church.

But this is not enough. This—let us quote the sacred words of this morning's Gospel with reverence—this " was said to them of old time." This was a message to your fathers and their fathers. But now "show we unto you a more excellent way." We point you to the pressing necessity, to the urgent peril of our own time. We point you to the great cities in which there dwell, in one sense together as countrymen and citizens, in another sense alone as strangers and almost aliens, the two representative men, the two classes, the two nations, " the one rich, and the other poor"; the one with his "exceeding many flocks and herds," his limitless enjoyments of every kind, bodily, intellectual, social, political, his traditions of comfort, his title-deeds of ascendency; and the other with his " nothing," his nothing " save one little ewe lamb," his per-

THE RICH AND THE POOR

sonal independence, his hard-won wage, his overgrown family, his house, as the greatest of your orators* put it, though the phrase is often irony, his "house which is his castle."

It is to these poor, yet citizens of no mean country and heirs of no mean responsibilities, that in these latter days the genius of your school guides you. It bids you renew in their service the old august Eton tradition. It says, Make it part of the Eton tradition in London, in Manchester, in Birmingham, in Leeds, in Liverpool, in every great centre of English life, to take the lead in brotherly service of the poor. Get to know them. Live some part of your lives among them. Look at life through their eyes as well as your own. Find out through their lips and from their looks, in friendly unstudied talk, how they think and feel on those great subjects on which your thoughts are so likely to be prejudices—property, land, taxation, labour, wages, houses, hours of work; service in the mine, the army, the navy; education of children, government by parties, the claims of freedom, the claims of religion. Of these difficult words there is not one, remember, which means only one thing. Look it out in the dictionary of accepted tradition,

* Lord Chatham.

it has one meaning; look it out in the dictionary of modern democracy, it has another. If a man in our day, and in the days which are at hand, would "serve his generation by the counsel of God," he must see, think, feel the facts of life in the language understanded of the people. Not by holding aloof, not by insisting on the exclusiveness, the fastidiousness, the direct privileges of his class, but by personal contact with other classes, personal observation, personal talk and, where possible, common action, he will best justify his claim to be "the first in service as the first in place."

Yes, my young friends, if I could speak to you to-day only as the friend of your order, only as the prudent interpreter of your aristocratic tradition, only as a timely adviser to set your house in order so as to be ready for the shocks, the roughnesses, the rudenesses of the coming age—even so I would counsel you to give a large and increasing part of your hearts to the life of the poor, and to return the loudest and most eager Yes to the eternal question, never more imperative and imperious than to-day, "Am I my brother's keeper?"

But, as I told you above, there is not only an Etonian reason for such work as is being done by your Mission and for your taking part in it; there

THE RICH AND THE POOR

is also a Christian reason. "He that hath ears to hear" this reason also, "let him hear." Happy is that boy and that young man who, early in life, can not only feel a natural respect for the poor and genially like them for their own sake, apart from any sense of public duty, but further can see in them the clients, the representatives, the very brothers of Jesus Christ. I know the danger of using such words lightly. "They flow," you say, "very readily from the lips of a preacher. He has only to take up his Bible and quote a little, and such titles are at once forthcoming. But if we boys were to use them, they would be with us 'cant.'"

Then, my friends, in God's name do not use them, do not use them yet. Anything better than this or any other kind of cant. Still do take note of the fact that there are others whom you can trust, to whom they are not cant. There are friends of your own, men who only a very few years back were boys here like yourselves, sitting where you sit at this hour, whose manner of life is just as free, simple, manly, unpretentious as your own. These men have given a part of their lives, and not a small part, to this very work which your Mission exists to foster. And what is curious and noteworthy is, you never find these men either bragging of it, or again getting tired of it and regretting that they have ever taken part in such illusion. Truly it is a case of *vestigia nulla retrorsum*. The West-end never goes to the East-end or to the North-east-end, and then, in the words of your great poet, casts some

> longing, lingering look behind.

No, your witnesses are men to be believed, and they tell you, one and all, that they have enjoyed, enjoyed keenly, the life they spent amidst the poor. They have learned so much from them. They have seen in them so much to admire; so much courage, patience, hope, dignity; so much that makes a nation great and a Church possible. And, further, they have found this life such a help to their own religious faith. They have seen in it so much of Christ—not so much talk about Him, or good works done daily in His name, but Christ Himself, His character, His influence, His enthusiasm, His self-devotion, His habit of unwearied prayer, His way of choosing disciples, His daily manner of life.

To such men, living such a life, it is no cant, but the simplest language they can use, to speak

THE RICH AND THE POOR

of the poor and needy as both the brothers and the representatives of Jesus Christ, and it is because they look upon them with this faith that they serve them with such persistency.

My young friends, I leave these thoughts with you. They are, I must believe, Christian thoughts. It is really never too early to get a hint, an appeal, a personal summons from Christ. It would not be strange, it would not be unlike Him, if He were this very day to put into the heart of one and another among you to devote his life largely, perhaps specially, to the service of the poor. No one knows when, or how, such a call may come.

Not many years ago I was walking at Harrow with the old Lord Shaftesbury. His son was present, no one else. Another much-loved son had died at the school more than thirty years before, and we went to the brow of the hill to see his grave. As we came back, and passed the school gates, the old man—he was nearly eighty—suddenly stopped, as if he saw something in the road, and pointing to it, said to his son: "It was just there that some sixty years ago I saw two drunken men carrying a pauper from the workhouse to his grave. The pall hung loose over the coffin. They were singing some ribald song. I remember my feeling of horror and disgust. I believe it was largely that sight which led me, under God, to devote my life to the service of the poor. There is nothing which the poor feel so keenly as disrespect to their dead."

That was how the call came, in part at least, in the days of his boyhood, to one famous Public School-man whose praise is in all the Churches. He lived to take an active and a delighted part in founding our Harrow Mission in London which seeks the same high objects as your own. Almost every public school has chosen for itself some such form of doing good. Surely it is a sign of the times, and a sign of good. We are not better than our fathers, but God has granted us to see visions which would have amazed them a hundred, seventy, fifty, even twenty years ago. Yes, God, who hath made of one blood all nations and all classes of men, and hath given to some favoured classes and families all things richly to enjoy, hath in these latter days spoken in parables to these favoured ones, even to the youngest among them, teaching them to see that the delight of personal enjoyment is as nothing compared with the delight of consecrated service, and that no society is safe, and no nation is sound, and no Church is Christ-

THE RICH AND THE POOR

like, and no school is true to the innermost spirit of its most exalted traditions, if it hears unmoved that old tale which once startled the slumbering conscience of a king, "There were two men in one city, the one rich and the other poor."

BLUSTER AND FAITH

Rugby School,
 Preached in the School
 Chapel on July 5, 1896.

Thou comest to me with a sword, and with a spear, and with a javelin; but I come to thee in the name of the Lord of Hosts, the God of the armies of Israel, which thou hast defied.

1 SAM. xvii. 45.

BLUSTER AND FAITH

THOU comest to me with every earthly weapon of attack, everything which can daunt the eye and wound the body. I come to thee in the name of "Him who is invisible," in the name of truth and reverence and piety. I come in the name of the God of my fathers, whose faith and obedience thou darest to deride.

There is not a boy here who does not know the undying story of David's victory over Goliath. We may safely predict that it can never lose its power to stir. What I want you, my friends, to see is how it is a type of every victory of good over evil.

On the one side are the big battalions, on the other side is a tender conscience. There, you look out on brute force, menace, outrageous insult. The Philistine curses David by his gods. He lets loose upon him every vulgar prejudice and every worldly maxim which he and his set have been content to deify.

But here, on the other side, you see the quiet intruder, perhaps the young intruder. He marvels at the universal panic. He smiles at the curses of the popular idols. In a moment his resolution is taken. "Let no man's heart fail; thy servant will go and fight with this Philistine."

My friends, is this all ancient history? Have you seen nothing of it in your school life, either when you first left home or even after you became members of this great and famous school?

In one of his delightful Canterbury sermons, preached nearly forty years ago, Dean Stanley, whom in this chapel I name with loving reverence, speaks of Christian chivalry as *the* great school virtue. "The duty," he says, "the privilege let me rather call it, of protecting the weak, of saving the innocent, of guiding the doubtful, of keeping down and driving away the tempter and the persecutor, this is 'the very religion of schoolboys.'"

Admirably true, and beautifully put; only let us make an addition—which Stanley of all men would eagerly have approved—the duty of protesting against evil, of standing up against wrong, in spite of all its brag and its bluster; this too

BLUSTER AND FAITH

is a large part of "the very religion of schoolboys."

Yes, allow as we may for all the blessed advances that the cause of Christ makes in the best schools, I do not believe that the time will ever come when this part of school religion will be obsolete. Even the best school will always have its Goliaths and sorely need its Davids. There will always be from time to time some set of boys, dreaded for their strength or age or dulness, who are known to be supporters of some bad custom—as drinking, or gambling, or copying, or lying to a master. No one pretends to think the custom right, and few in their hearts like it. The more religious are shocked by it; the more fastidious think it "bad form."

But there it is, backed by power, heralded by bluster, with "a man," as it were, "bearing a shield" going before it.

And then some one has the courage to speak out. He does not argue. Perhaps he is not clever enough for that. But no amount of numbers or of swagger or of brandished weapons can make him either respect or dread what his home and his mother and his ripening conscience have declared to be wrong. Instantly he protests. He does not put his protest into Bible words; he never dreams of being a hero; but, without knowing it, without dreaming of it, he is acting once more the true heroic part which once found a voice in one of the sublime voices of history: "Thou comest to me with a sword, and with a spear, and with a javelin; but I come to thee in the name of the Lord of hosts, the God of the armies of Israel, which thou hast defied."

Oh, my friends, may the Almighty Father ever help, may men and women ever applaud and encourage, may boys ever in their heart of hearts admire and revere all these priceless champions of the sanctities and the pieties of youthful life. Their worth to a school is simply incalculable.

It was of one of these that Arnold once said, in words often quoted, and here, I suppose, almost proverbial: "I would stand to that man hat in hand." It was of one of these that Arnold must have been thinking when, at the close of one of his best-known sermons, preached more than sixty years ago, he quoted Milton's glorious lines on the Seraph Abdiel:

> The Seraph Abdiel, faithful found
> Among the faithless, faithful only he. . . .

BLUSTER AND FAITH

> Servant of God, well done! Well hast thou fought
> The better fight, who singly hast maintained
> Against revolted multitudes the cause
> Of truth, in word mightier than they in arms.

It was of the earlier sermons of Arnold from this pulpit that a well-known pen has written: "And so . . . was brought home to the young boy, for the first time, the meaning of his life: that it was no fool's or sluggard's paradise into which he had wandered by chance, but a battlefield ordained from of old, where there are no spectators, but the youngest must take his side, and the stakes are life and death."

Yes, it is not in the Chapel of Rugby that we can ever lose sight of that eternal ever-changing "battle-field" where Israel stands shivering on one side and the Philistines stand bragging on the other side, and "there is a valley between them." Only, dear friends, let me just warn you that this image of the battlefield, stirring as it is, may at times mislead. It is not the most giantlike evils which are always the most dangerous. Again and again, if we really hate evil, and long to fight it, we must long also to see it more plainly. We would give much at times to see across a clearly marked valley some giant form stalking about with sword and spear. It is the very absence of this downright avowed defiance that often makes the task of the Christian champion so difficult.

It was something of this kind that your own great poet* was feeling when he wrote, not many years after leaving Rugby,

>What are we to resist, and what are we to be friends with?
>Yet is my feeling rather to ask, Where *is* the battle?
>O that the armies indeed were arrayed! O joy of the onset!
>Sound, thou Trumpet of God, come forth, Great Cause, to array us,
>King and Leader appear, thy soldiers sorrowing seek thee,
>Would that the armies indeed were arrayed, O where is the battle?

Yes, the Davids of our day have to fight at times very subtle foes. They have to make out who these foes are, and where they are, and how much of their artillery is pointed against the Ark of God. Telescope and telegraph have to be patiently employed before the bulk of the unseen antagonist can be made to loom large. For instance, is a new novel or a new poem impious and dangerous? Is it an insult to God? Is it an outrage on decency and piety? Or is it only partly this and partly something very different? There may be much beauty and tenderness in it, much appeal to moral instinct. How much here is of the host of

* Arthur Hugh Clough.

the Philistine? How much of the army of the living God? Is there a Goliath here at all? If so, the old coarse defiance has strangely toned down. We hear no more the brutal challenge, "Come to me, and I will give thy flesh to the beasts of the field." It is rather, "Let me come over to thee, and I will find something even in thy time-worn God to admire."

Ay, the Philistine of our day has learned to borrow the language of Israel. He comes to David, if he find any David to confront him, not always with sword and spear and javelin, but with smooth words and diplomatic deference, as if the foul Dagon of Ashdod were willing, for a consideration, to compliment and patronize the Jehovah of Shiloh.

My friends, the more veiled the approach of the enemy, the more need there is for the good soldier of Christ to be on his guard. "Ye shall know them by their fruits." A little wise foresight, a little careful inquiry, a little watchful observation of results, will enable you to see whether you are dealing with a friend or a foe; whether there is a valley between your two positions; whether, indeed, to quote Arthur Clough once more, there *is* a battle.

And when you have decided, by every instinct and by every act of reason, that there is indeed a battle, and that the moment has come when you must either "confess" Christ before men or "deny" Him, then let me offer you one more word of counsel. As Goliath in our days so often lays aside his material weapons—his sword, and spear, and javelin—so also at times must David. We love to think of—nay, to see across the ages—the heroic Shepherd-boy putting off from him the heavy coat of mail with which convention had thought to protect him. We love to see him, with his favourite sling in his hand, stepping down coolly to the brook in the valley, and there, in full view of the two wondering armies, choosing carefully his five smooth stones, each a sure messenger of death. We love to see him, still himself—not Saul, nor Abner, nor even Jonathan—trusting solely to the weapons of his boyhood, the weapons which God had blessed before in many a youthful encounter.

But when we come to turn the history into allegory, and to ask ourselves, "How can I do in my day what David did so gloriously in his?" then the scene is shifted. There is no visible fight, either of strength or of skill. The five

BLUSTER AND FAITH

smooth stones may rest in the brook. The sling may be replaced in the little home armoury. There will be no whiz through the air of the first and smoothest of the stones, no heavy collapse of the befooled and belated giant. No, the weapons of our modern Davids are mostly, as St. Paul said of his own, "not of the flesh." More often they take the form of redoubled prayer, of gentle but firm speech, of a sudden blush of shame, of a startled frown of indignation, of something which says, or at least implies, "My gods are not as thy gods, my principles are not as thine, my language and customs shall not be as thine. Thou comest to me in the name of the world and of the world's latest sophism—clever, audacious, but cynical and godless—but I come to thee in the name of home and faith and piety and purity, which are indeed, so my conscience tells me, the consecrated armies of the living God."

But oh, my young friends, when we talk of moral fighting, when we spur ourselves to the front by phrases and images drawn from the battlefield, let us never forget that the first and hardest victory is the victory over self. The David of the battlefield is the David of his father's sheepfolds. The conqueror of Goliath is the boy-conqueror of the lion and the bear. It was in those long silent hours in the pastures of Bethlehem, hours of the day and hours of the night, that David learned his two life-lessons, and even he learned them only imperfectly—to know his own weakness, and to "stay upon his God." If we are to fight evil, evil must see and recognise that we are good. And God must see it also, and good men must see it also.

There is something very glorious and animating, especially in the days of our youth, in the two great visions of combat—first the vision of fighting, as a child and as a man, "under Christ's banner against sin, the world, and the devil"; and then the vision of the armies which are in heaven following upon white horses Him that is called faithful and true.

No Christian boy, I believe, passes through boyhood without at least once seeing these champions, however far off, and longing some day to do as they have done and to be where they are.

> And would we join that blest array,
> And follow in the might
> Of Him, the Faithful and the True,
> In raiment clean and white?

BLUSTER AND FAITH

> How can we fight for Truth and God,
> Enthralled to lies and sin ?
> He who would wage such war on earth
> Must first be true within.

So wrote one of the most beloved of your own champions,* beloved far beyond your own borders. His statue will soon stand in your midst, to remind you of the faithful witness which he bore both to the teaching of his youth at Rugby and to the lessons of his manhood learned in many a hard campaign.

I cannot better close what I have tried to urge than in his own truly Christian and most manly prayer. May each of us, man and boy, strive to make it his own prayer as long as life may last !

> O God of Truth ! for whom we long,
> O Thou that hearest prayer,
> Do Thine own battle in our hearts,
> And slay the falsehood there.
> So, tried in Thy refining fire,
> From every lie set free,
> In us Thy perfect Truth shall dwell,
> And we may fight for Thee !

* Thomas Hughes.

PUBLIC SCHOOL "ESPRIT DE CORPS"

BROMSGROVE SCHOOL,
 Preached in the Parish Church on the
 Commemoration Day, July 27, 1898.

O pray for the peace of Jerusalem: they shall prosper that love thee.

Peace be within thy walls, and plenteousness within thy palaces.

For my brethren and companions' sakes, I will wish thee prosperity.

Yea, because of the house of the Lord our God I will seek to do thee good.—PSALM CXXII. 6-9.

PUBLIC SCHOOL *ESPRIT DE CORPS*

IT is a Psalm that all men love, and specially, I think, men from Public Schools. When it comes round naturally at a school festival, as it does to-day, it almost compels us to listen to its voice. And the compulsion is certainly "not grievous," the thoughts, the words, the melody, the music are all so tender and so beautiful.

We will take them just as they are. We will not stop to trace their history. Whatever was meant by "Songs of Degrees" or "Songs of Ascent," it is plain that this group of lovely songs has a common source, and that the keynote to them all is religious patriotism. "God is in the midst of them all," the God of the nation, the God of the fathers, the God who has at last "turned again the captivity of Sion," and made His way-worn travellers "like unto them that dream."

Then, again, Jerusalem, the more than ever Holy

City, is the centre of all hearts, the centre of joy and hope and love and united worship : "I was glad when they said unto me, Let us go into the house of the Lord."

It is strange how these old Hebrew songs, so joyous, though at times so mournful, fit into our English hearts on a day like this. By a sure instinct we claim them as our own. They were written, we feel, not only for our "learning," but for our delight and our pride. They minister not only to soft and tender emotions, but to strong and manly passions, and among the "strong passions" of these latter days is one which is more or less new in man's history; I mean the *esprit de corps*—there is as yet no English word for it—the *esprit de corps* of our Public Schools.

There is, of course, no trace of this feeling in ancient life, whether Hebrew, Oriental, Greek or Roman. In modern life there is little or no trace of it on the Continent, or, except quite latterly, even in America. Nay, even in England you will scarcely find it, as an active visible power, till, say, the last century and a half. How little mark has it left on literature till the time of Gray's famous Ode some hundred and fifty years ago ! Winchester, Eton, Westminster, and other great

PUBLIC SCHOOL "ESPRIT DE CORPS"

foundations have, of course, been striking their roots deeper and deeper for five hundred, four hundred, three hundred years, and during all that time boy-friendships must have been made as warm, as joyous, as full of romance as those which kindle your hearts to-day. But if you come to think of it, how few of these friendships have become in any way noteworthy before our century! How few of them have found expression in song, in fiction, in essays, in sermons!

There are, no doubt, exceptions. Some of you may remember the touching poem,* *How Lord Nairn was Saved.* He was one of the Jacobite rebels of 1716. He was condemned with five others, who were all sent to the block. The new foreign king, George the First, and his strong-willed minister, Sir Robert Walpole, were determined that the man should die. But the warrant for his death could not take effect without the signature of the Secretary of State, General Stanhope, and Stanhope positively refused to have a hand in killing his old Eton friend.

Let me quote a few words from the poem, which should be better known :

* By Sir Francis Doyle. See *Poet's Walk*, p. 308.

> I brook on this point no control,
>   He shouted: Seek not to reply;
> For, by that God who made the soul,
>   I will not have him die.
> What, use me, ruthless, as a tool,
>   To slay my earliest friend? Our names
> Are cut together in the school,
>   Together at my dame's:
> Half of my past is his, half his is mine;
> I will not hear it argued—I resign.

That threat of resignation saved the forfeited life. It is, so far as I know, the first recorded instance of schoolboy *esprit de corps*.

If we look on another sixty or seventy years, we shall find Wellesley and Canning at Eton, and the shy William Cowper at Westminster, full of ardour for their great schools.

Cowper, who had been the comrade of Warren Hastings, cannot, will not believe, whatever Burke and Sheridan may say, that the friend he knew

> to be so gentle then,
> Has grown a villain and the worst of men.

It is about this time that we begin to trace the growth of this school *esprit de corps*, not very much more than a hundred years ago. What Gray did for Eton, and Byron fifty years later for Harrow, had scarcely been attempted before. The truth,

PUBLIC SCHOOL "ESPRIT DE CORPS"

I suppose, is that the great schools, happy and powerful as they were, had hardly yet become self-conscious. They lived, as it were, without knowing it. In our time, school after school has had its Tercentenary Festival, and younger schools have had their first Jubilee; but last century, whatever be the cause, I do not read of Bicentenaries and the like. It looks as if some centuries of quiet growth were needed before that strange, delightful institution, an English public school, could awaken into proud self-consciousness, and almost marvel at its own *esprit de corps*.

And now, my friends, I ask you to notice just two roots, if we may so express it, of this *esprit de corps*. I seem to find them both, distinct as they are, in the words of this morning's Psalm. The one root is this: "For my brethren and companions' sakes, I will wish thee prosperity." The other root is a kind of amendment on the first, not in any way displacing it but grafting upon it something fresh and something precious: "Yea, because of the house of the Lord our God I will seek to do thee good."

As to the first, I can imagine a grave voice saying, "It was said to them of old time"; and as to the second, "But I say unto you." In a word, the one ideal, genuine and charming as it is, is short of Christian. The other ideal is Christian, or it is nothing.

I have often thought, and sometimes said, on occasions such as this, that the old ideal, the ideal which satisfied "them of old time," was beautifully and almost adequately expressed in a famous epitaph now nearly sixty years old.

If ever you pay a visit to Eton, and enter the northern side chapel, look for the tablet put up by Arthur Duke of Wellington to his illustrious eldest brother, Richard, Marquess Wellesley, one of the greatest of the many great rulers of India. Lord Wellesley, a brilliant classical scholar, wrote some ten lines in Latin to be placed upon his tomb. They record what he considered his debt to the dear fostering mother of his aspiring boyhood.

Listen to a rough paraphrase of just a few of them, and ask yourselves, while I repeat it, whether it does not fairly give the old, less than Christian, ideal of what a public school can teach :

> To follow greatness with supreme desire,
> The beckoning peaks of glory to admire,
> In youth's clear dawn to gaze with sober eye
> On the chaste splendours of the classic sky;
> True praise to love, false vulgar praise to flee—
> Such were the lessons that I learned from thee.

PUBLIC SCHOOL "ESPRIT DE CORPS"

If this were all that a great school could give us, even then, I think, we might well say to each other on a day of thanksgiving, "For my brethren and companions' sakes, I will wish thee prosperity." Even here the *esprit de corps*, though short of its highest, is "a thing of beauty and a joy for ever," of power to mould character and inspire careers.

But is it all, or is it anything like all ? Is there not something beyond, of which "the house of the Lord our God" is "the symbol and the instrument," something which has become, thank God, an essential part of public school life ? When we say to ourselves, as so many Public School-boys now say to themselves in their graver hours all over England, as many of you, my friends, old and young, are, I am sure, saying from your hearts to-day, "Because of the house of the Lord our God I will seek to do thee good," what is this new element which by slow degrees has stolen into the very notion of a school's prosperity ? What is this new thing that would hardly have been thought of in the school days of George Herbert at Westminster, or Sir Philip Sidney at Shrewsbury, or Sheridan at Harrow, or the mighty Chatham at Eton ?

The new thing is this—the conception, the

growth, the sight of a Christian life at school, not in spite of school and school's many temptations, but fostered by school work, and school discipline, and school organisation, and school games, and school worship, and so gradually but surely by school example and school tradition. This is not only a possible thing ; this has come to be the thing at which almost every school professes to aim. "First Christians, then gentlemen, then scholars." This order, laid down some sixty years ago by great and earnest men, such as Arnold and Wordsworth and Moberly and Vaughan, has come to be regarded as the one and only order that an enlightened conscience can tolerate. To invert the order would be treason to the "new creation."

Now of this highest of ideals, the Christian ideal, and this purest element of prosperity, Christian prosperity, what is the obvious symbol? You will all say with me, the "House of the Lord our God." We may use it, or half use it, or misuse it. We may use it so poorly that, when we leave School and go up to College, we may rejoice in our fancied emancipation. This, too, I have known and seen, and I would humbly ask my brother teachers to note it and learn wisdom

PUBLIC SCHOOL "ESPRIT DE CORPS"

from it; but that man does not know the Public Schools of England in this last half of the nineteenth century who has failed to see the mighty part played by the school "house of God," be it cathedral, or abbey, or chapel, or parish church, in comforting, lifting, purifying, moulding the character of young and happy boys between twelve and nineteen years of age. And if so, then a man must be perverse, or cynical, if, kneeling to-day in this house of God, and recalling the life of this school during the last twenty-five years, he can satisfy his hopes for its welfare by any prayer less lofty, less Christian, than this, not only, beautiful as it is, "For my brethren and companions' sakes, I will wish thee prosperity," but also something more, something higher and something deeper: "Yea, because of the house of the Lord our God I will seek to do thee good."

Christian friends, you must have looked forward, many of you, to this day. It is a landmark in your history, a landmark both in personal life and in school life. It is charged, charged to the full, with both private and public feeling. It looks forward as well as backward. If I may say so, it "abounds in hope." You know how much of heart and brain and spirit has been devoted to your school during the past twenty-five years. You have seen the steps of advance, firmly set, never recalled, and you know that the advance is even now, even to-day, advancing. If at such a time some voices of earthly personal praise and congratulation are inevitable, you would wish to crown, if not to replace, them by something yet better and truer and more deeply set, and therefore far more valued—the example of one great teacher and administrator, who summed up some thirty years of his wonderful life by saying : " I count not myself yet to have apprehended; but one thing I do, forgetting the things which are behind, and straining, stretching forward to the things which are before, I press on toward the goal unto the prize of the high calling of God in Christ Jesus." *

A man who is fired by this noble ambition has his own standard of the "prosperity" of a loved society. As long as life may last, one thing is certain—for the sake of the house of the Lord our God he will seek to do it good.

* Ep. to the Philippians iii. 13.

IN MEMORIAM

HARROW SCHOOL,
 Spoken on March 19, 1895, in
 Memory of Frederick Ponsonby,
 Sixth Earl of Bessborough.

Q

IN MEMORIAM

IT is, I suppose, the first time that any service like this has been held in this chapel, and yet it has been built nearly sixty years. The friend whom we have lost had already left school for Cambridge when it first rose from the ground. How amazed he would have been if he had then been told, "The voice of the Burial Service will never be heard within these walls till, some sixty years hence, Harrow men and Harrow boys meet there together to offer *you* their last farewell."

There are some kinds of affection and respect for which length of days is necessary. Not indeed that we need live many years, or many months, or even many weeks, to create intense and undying affection. I often think that our memorial tablets in this chapel, really a unique collection, bear touching witness to the preciousness and loveableness of boy life. We have records there of life closing at every age, I think, from thirteen to eighteen. Each of those early deaths darkened a happy home, and not one of them failed to touch many hearts among ourselves. As the bell tolled out in the night air, we said good-bye with real affection and regret to one of ourselves, one of our young family, whom not a few here had loved.

And now the bell has tolled for one of the very oldest amongst us, and we feel that a long life was needed to give him that peculiar place in our hearts which is the cause of this unexampled gathering to-day.

The oldest master here was not born when he began that series of constant visits which ended barely a fortnight since. When I came here as a boy, more than forty-eight years ago, "Ponsonby and Grimston" were already an institution. Every summer brought them to us three days at least in the week, and the oldest among us could not have told when the custom had begun. So far as I know, there was then nothing like it in any other public school. I do not, of course, mean that other schools had not equally inspired deep and romantic affection in one chosen son after another;

IN MEMORIAM

but the peculiar note of this affection was that it was shown by constant presence. It was always, as they say, "in evidence." One year followed another, one generation followed another, new masters came, and new boys; still "Ponsonby and Grimston" were one of the traditions, one of the weekly sights—as I said, one of the established institutions of Harrow life.

First, one of the two friends was taken from us, and now the other has gone. What shall we say of him in this house of God, this house in which he so often came to worship?

Only the very simplest things and the very truest. How he would have hated anything far-fetched or overstrained!

He was a very modest and a very simple man. He knew the world well, but somehow he kept himself, or rather, God kept him, "unspotted" from it. He cared indeed for not a few public causes, and he was a favourite in every society, but his heart, every one knew, was here. Himself a childless man, he found in the young life of Harrow boys something that satisfied his heart and kept him young. He knew that he was serving the school by coming among us as he did. It was a new and original kind of service. Early instinct had prompted it, and experience had proved that his instinct was right.

He touched our life chiefly, as we all know, on one side, its athletic side. Every one is saying—how many must have said it to-day!—"The cricket-ground will never look the same again now he is gone." It is easily said, but it is felt also, and it is true. That long-tried devotion, that eye of calm, gentle, penetrating scrutiny, that beautiful self-suppression even when advising or criticising, gave a charm to the cricket-ground even beyond its own. Those games of ours which he had so long watched were his educators as well as yours. They brought out in him rare gifts both of insight and of sympathy. He was always on the look-out for athletic promise, but still more for character. If there was one thing that he specially loved, it was to "comfort the feeble-minded," to help a boy to believe again in himself when bad luck or ill-health or any other disaster had dashed his spirits and made him despondent. I feel as certain as if I had heard and read them all myself, that if we could have a record of the words and the letters of sympathy that he spoke or wrote to Harrow boys at critical moments in their school fortunes, it would surprise us by its depth and volume. The getting into the eleven, the just missing it, the being cut out at the last moment by some one who till then had been hardly thought of, the successive failures match after match, the half-meditated resignation, the brilliant success just in time ; or, again, the sudden illness, the sudden accident, the slackness in some part of the field, the need of stricter discipline and greater energy and "pulling all together"; the necessity of keeping down all petty jealousies, even house jealousies, and thinking of nothing but the good of the dear old school—these were our friend's opportunities. These were the moments when his eye, his voice, his pen "took the field." I shall be surprised if there are not hundreds of Harrow men who still keep, deeply treasured in their memory, some such note, or some such quiet word, of which the substance was, "Never mind ; don't lose heart ; try again."

But there is another word to be spoken of his connexion with our games. He saw, and loved to see, all their charm and all their educating power, but he saw their danger also ; and the danger lay chiefly in this—not that they led some boys here and there to be idle in school work, but that they dazzled too much the Harrow imagination, satisfied too easily Harrovian ambition, tempted both boys and men to look on athletic achievement as the main honour of the school, and tended to chill by comparison, or at least to overlay, the yet nobler fire of intellectual enthusiasm.

It was with this feeling—I am sure it was so in the one case, I believe it was so in the other—that he instituted both his Scholarship and his Prize. As to the Scholarship, he must have felt that its value lay largely in its coming from himself, himself the recognised champion of all athletic excellence; and as to the Prize, this was beyond doubt its object, for he wished it to be given to such member or members of the eleven as had shown most diligence in their school work. There may be some now in this chapel who have gained that Prize. They and all who ever gained it will be thinking of him to-day. They valued it chiefly because it brought them into direct sympathy with its kind giver. Each "Ponsonby prizeman" knew that he had done the very thing, in honest intellectual work, which Lord Bessborough, the great cricketer and judge of cricket, wished the whole school to aim at. Whether that Prize be permanent or not, I do not know. Whether it

IN MEMORIAM

would do its work equally well, or well at all, now that he is gone, it is not for me to judge. But the fact that he gave the Prize, with this object in view, during so many years, should, I think, never be forgotten; for it is much more than a prize, it is really part of our dear friend's mind and character and legacy.

I have said more than I intended, yet another word shall be said, and it shall be said truly. Perhaps, from the nature of the case, only two other men living could say it so emphatically. A man who comes down year after year, and week after week, to take a leading part in our games must necessarily wield, as time goes on, a marked influence. He influences the boys both while they are in the school and after they have left. This influence need not necessarily be a good one; it might be a bad one. To me it is a joyful thing on this solemn day, when one would not willingly use one glozing word, to bear my public testimony to this dear old friend, not only as an old Harrovian who loved and admired him, but as a responsible Master who watched his constantly increasing influence, that it was, so long as I observed it, admirable. In fact you cannot think of him here, you cannot see him on the cricket-ground, alone or with a group round him, you cannot see him slowly walking up the hill, or standing at the school gate, or staying the Sunday at the house of one of the masters, or worshipping in this house of God, or kneeling at the Lord's Table, without thinking also of what is pure and healthy and upright and generous. It is a blessing that we have had such a man, and that we have had him so long—long enough to love him ourselves, and to let him know that he was loved.

Just ten years ago, on his seventieth birthday, some of us surprised him with a birthday gift. Perhaps it was a reminder that he was becoming old, but anyhow it was a reminder that there were many who loved him. I was unable, to my great regret, to be present on the day that he received it, but I was told that he could not speak, he was so much moved. He felt as many of us are feeling to-day, and we are not the only mourners. Far away in Ireland, even as we speak, they are carrying him to his last home among the graves of his fathers. There, too, and not only in that one part of Ireland, he was warmly loved. He was, in fact, the model Irish landlord, kindly, sympathetic, intelligent, genial, humorous—above all, just, with a strong sense of his responsibilities. His tenants

IN MEMORIAM

there will find it hard to imagine what we English boys and men are thinking of him here to-day at his old English school. Perhaps it is almost as difficult for us to share their special reverence and regret. Only we all love him.

What shall be our last word? The memories of the best-loved men pass rapidly away. A man, whose face, whose word, whose will, whose charm is in every heart to-day, is within three years almost unknown to a new generation of the young. So it will be with this dear friend, who for sixty years has borne a foremost part in every enterprise for the good of Harrow, who, in every change of our fortunes, has given us so much—money, time, counsel, sympathy, friendship—and above all has, without a break, given us himself. No project had a chance of success without Ponsonby's support. No gathering was complete without Ponsonby's presence. This is the last such gathering. To some of us he seems more present now than ever. In a few years you boys, and those who come after you, will have but a few vague memories of him—the Scholarship, the picture in the library, some picture, doubtless, on the cricket-ground, it may be some memorial bearing his name, and then the legend, the gradually growing legend of the two friends—so unlike each other, so lovable separately, so singularly attractive when taken together—who for so many decades of years were always seen in all weathers in our favourite place of resort. Let us hope that the Harrow boys of the long years to come will so far read that legend aright as to hate the things which the two friends hated, and love what they loved; to hate slackness, and swagger, and show-off, and ill-temper, and selfishness, and the wretched notion of "each man for himself," or again, each house for itself; and to love, as they so cordially loved, whether in victory or defeat, thoroughness, fairness, modesty, hopefulness, the "rules of the game," the "umpire's decision final," chivalry, generosity, courtesy to opponents, public spirit, the spirit of comradeship, the spirit of "Auld Lang Syne," the spirit which, here and in every ancient society, enables "brethren to dwell together in unity."

You know how on our Founder's Day the long and ever-lengthening list of Benefactors is read out to us before the last hymn, and at the end the reader pauses for a moment, and then says, in the name of all present, "Let us give thanks." Is not this a kind of Commemoration Day? Have we not been to-day commemorating one of the truest and most warm-hearted Benefactors that our school has ever known ? Let us then turn from man to God, from the gift, so long given and now so tenderly withdrawn, to the Giver of every good gift, and let me say, in your name and in the name of hundreds of our brothers in every part of the world, " Let us give thanks."

THE ATTRACTION OF THE CROSS

St. Paul's, Knightsbridge,
 Preached during the London
 Mission, February 14, 1885.

I, if I be lifted up from the earth, will draw all men unto me.—St. John xii. 32.

THE ATTRACTION OF THE CROSS

THE truth of the words has been proved ever since. There has been and there is no spiritual magnet like the Cross. Those who are proof against every other attraction are overcome by this. It touches one man in one way, another in another. From one it draws tears; from another, thought; from a third, adoration; from a fourth, vehement action; from each man according to the bent of his character. But no man who has any spiritual life in him can stand beneath the Cross quite unmoved. If the saying were not as true now as ever, this Mission would never have been thought of, and we, Christian friends, should not have been here to-day. We are here because we believe that the Cross has a message for us—for us as well as for others.

It is somewhat of a novel thought that there should be a Mission to educated men. The name of a Mission excites very different feelings in different minds. To some it suggests all that is holy and hopeful and prophetic—Christ Himself, His love, His power, His purposes, His victory; the earth "full of the knowledge of the Lord as the waters cover the sea." To others it suggests not Christ, but feeble Christians, the sickly shibboleth of a worn-out creed, spasmodic and short-lived enthusiasm, credulous superstition, discredited prophecy.

But one thing we may safely say, that, whenever hitherto we have thought about Missions, we have thought of them as meant not for ourselves, but for others. We have thought of them, if I may so say, *de haut en bas*, as meant for outcasts of some kind—barbarous tribes, heathen fanatics, fallen women, Arabs of the streets, "waifs and strays," and the like. Without intending to be Pharisaical, we have hardly dreamed of a Mission to the upper classes, to the men of light and leading and fashion, to the club and the drawing-room and the family pew, as well as to the foul alley and the clattering street and the "bitter cry" of the destitute, often the more bitter because it is not a cry, but only a dumb, brooding, unconscious acquiescence.

THE ATTRACTION OF THE CROSS

But this Mission has spoken to us also—to us Public School men, and others who are like ourselves. This, as I understand it, is the meaning of these services in this church. This is my sole warrant for appearing before you, Christian brethren, this evening. It has fallen to my lot, during twenty-five years of happy labour, to see some four thousand young boys of the upper classes come under my official notice, besides those whom I knew when I was a boy myself. The great proportion of these are, of course, now men, holding, many of them, positions more or less conspicuous in the professions, in business, in literature, in the army—ay, in the army. It has been given me to see bright careers opening there, and bright careers swiftly closed. Only last Sunday I was reminding my own boys, in their chapel, that Earle, my own contemporary, one of the merriest boys I ever remember, was entrusted with the proud but perilous distinction of leading one of the chief armies of rescue. And now, before another Sunday, he too lies in a soldier's grave, like Burnaby and St. Vincent and so many others; and—such is the tie of brotherhood that binds all Public Schools—I know, my friends, that there is not a man here, to whatever school he belongs, who does not, even while I speak, feel with me for our losses, as I in my heart should assuredly feel for his.

Well, brethren, this Mission comes now to all of us, bound to one another by this common tie, which at this moment, at the end of this solemn week, seems to us, I dare to say, more sacred than it ever seemed before. We see now that it is not solely a delightful social bond, but a Christian bond also; and we ask ourselves whether it may not indeed be a "power from on high," working for Christ and for Christ's "little ones."

And how does the voice of this Mission find us? I can, of course, in these few minutes deal, and that most cursorily, with but a few imagined cases.

1. It finds, I suppose, some of us living lives of downright sin. Shall we suppose that all such sinners are outside these walls, that not a single man here is yielding his soul and his body as a slave to sin? I can hardly believe it. True, men in our rank of life seldom go through those visible paroxysms of remorse which startle us, for example, in the wonderful ministries of Wesley and Whitefield a hundred and fifty years ago; but we, too, have our agonies of shame, at once the clear

vision and the enfeebled grasp of the good and the pure. We have—who is so strong a swimmer as never to have known it?—we have our drowning clutch after better things. The old Psalmist was the spokesman not only of poor illiterate outcasts, when he said in his self-mission to himself, "My sins have taken such hold upon me that I am not able to look up." No! There must be many a man here, whether clergyman or layman, who can say, and does say, without a shadow of affectation, "We are tied and bound with the chain of our sins; the remembrance of them is grievous unto us, the burthen of them is intolerable."

"I, if I be lifted up from the earth, will draw all men unto me." This is Christ's answer to all such genuine self-abasement. Compared with this, what answer is worth anything? Supposing that I, or any physician of the soul, could tell you, with the minute analysis of medical science, "This is how your sickness began. This is where you took the infection. It was there, perhaps very early in childhood, that you breathed that foul miasma; since then it has never quite worked itself out of your constitution. You must put yourself under regimen. You must fill up vacant hours and minutes. You must pre-occupy those mysterious and perilous intervals of rest and respite—this week, perhaps, is one of them—when the unclean spirit is gone out of you, and is seeking fresh homes elsewhere. You must give up this or that indulgence. You must adopt this or that spiritual exercise,"—suppose, I say, I could thus feel your spirit's pulse, and make a full diagnosis of your moral system, showing that I read you through and through, what help would that give you to compare for one moment with that voice of authority which goes straight to the heart from one Physician alone—" I am hanging on the cross for sin—for your sins and such as yours. I have power on earth to forgive sins. I draw all men unto me. Go, and sin no more" ?

II. But perhaps the sinfulness to which we plead guilty may be of a different kind. Some of us might perhaps say, as poor Nelson said, while he lay dying from the fatal shot, " I have not been a great sinner ;" but which of us would dream of denying—which of us Public School men would dream of denying—that we have been terribly worldly, living lives on a low level, which seem a sort of affront to the truth when we go quietly and honestly to our Bible and read what Christ said, or turn to the lives of really holy men and women, and see what a grand thing they made of temptations vanquished and battles won?

Every now and then some one speaks to his own generation with a prophet's voice, and makes them feel their worldliness. Nearly ninety years have passed since the world of fashion and of politics was startled and almost scandalized by a prophet-voice of this kind. It was the voice, not of a bishop, or a clergyman, or an ascetic of any kind, but of a brilliant orator and a dazzling favourite of society—the man of whom Pitt declared that no man possessed in so high a degree the gift of natural eloquence; the man of whom Madame de Staël once said, " You told me I should meet the most devout of men; you did not tell me that I should also meet the wittiest." You will see that I am speaking of the illustrious William Wilberforce and his " Practical View of Christianity," the book which, in its day, was a kind of West-End Mission, speaking to men of the world, to men and women of society, to statesmen, and lawyers, and physicians, and soldiers, and clergymen, pointing them affectionately to the words and example of Christ and

His Apostles, and asking them, in the spirit not of censoriousness or of satire but of brotherly charity, whether, if that standard were true, their own lives were Christian or pagan.

To us, brethren, of this generation, at all events of this solemn and pathetic week—a week such as neither we nor our fathers have known—another prophetic voice makes, though in different accents, the same searching appeal. It comes from the heroic soldier whose character is now part of the nation's treasure, and even of that more precious inheritance which is in the keeping of All Saints' Day. What does Gordon say to us men of the world? "While the world is in the state it now is, there would be no one so unwelcome to come to reside in it as Christ. He would be dead against (say) nearly all our pursuits, and be altogether *outré*."

Allow as much as you will, as much as your reverence permits, for the rough force of this language of the soldier; substitute, if you will, for "nearly all our pursuits," some feebler paraphrase, such as "the spirit in which even our most innocent pursuits are in general carried on;" deduct as much as you please—and will you not even then allow this voice from Khartoum—this

THE ATTRACTION OF THE CROSS

prophet-voice, I will again dare to call it—to say to you, as the beloved Apostle said of old, " Love not the world, neither the things that are in the world : if any man love the world, the love of the Father is not in him " ?

Surely, surely, brethren—I say it to myself, God knows, at least as much as to you—surely we will not let this week pass by, we will not have listened to that noble voice of the dead, without praying God to stir us mightily in our worldly routine, and help us to lift up our poor lives to something worthier of the Christian name.

III. And if you ask me in what form this revival of our moribund life may be best re-cast, and how, when we shake off the fetters of worldliness, we may best move forwards as the freemen of Christ, I say, as one counsel—one only, but one which this generation needs sorely, and, thank God, is coming to welcome—realize the meaning of Christian brotherhood and its manifold responsibilities. Members as you all are of a privileged class, the class of birth, and comfort, and culture, and influence, "remember the poor." Give a new and a mightier life to that old maxim which I do not scruple to call the noblest legacy of feudal days, *Noblesse oblige.* Revive this maxim in the name of Jesus Christ. Away with the miserable notion that Christian brotherhood can be satisfied by a few guineas to this society and an occasional speech for another. " Do not even the publicans so ? " What we want, or rather, what Christ and His Gospel want, is something very different from this. The ancient watchword, *Noblesse oblige*, means, when Christianised and re-commissioned, lively sympathy, well-instructed study, frequent personal visits, large pecuniary sacrifices, well-planned schemes for that highest benevolence which teaches those who lack and suffer to respect and to trust themselves.

Brethren, I know that, in laying such thoughts before you, I am lifting up no shadowy ideal. Probably there are few among my hearers—those of them, I mean, who are Public School men—who are not already supporting some so-called Mission, conducted by the school which claims their love and homage. There are, of course, bad moral symptoms in the age in which we live. There are also, thank God, good symptoms. My own temperament, my own personal experience, lead me, force me, to look chiefly on the good. I would not, indeed, lay a flattering unction to the soul of any man, or of any school, or of any class. But I do say, it is a sight to cheer the hearts of all true servants of the Cross to know that within the last few years almost every Public School has established its Mission in some seat of suffering, or of squalor, or of ignorance; that the movement is bringing together schoolfellows of every rank and taste and pursuit, laying hold upon leading boys just before they leave their school, and predisposing them to join their elders a few years later in active participation in work for the poor.

Suffer me, brethren — pardon the apparent egotism—if I venture to go back in thought to a well-remembered day more than seventeen years ago, when it fell to my lot, in the chapel of my own beloved school, to impress upon those who were then boys some of the hopes and aspirations of a Founder's Day.

"Sometimes," I said, " I ask myself whether that spirit of intense union which binds together the boys of a great school during their school life might not naturally take the form of co-operation afterwards; whether they might not in after years draw the tie yet closer, and give it a fresh clearness and stringency by associating together, either by themselves or with kindred spirits of other schools, for works conducive to the public weal. It sometimes seems to me as though, from the peculiar constitution of these schools—the wealth of many of their members, their generosity, their chivalry, their great social ascendency, their habits of self-government, their love of liberty, and their reverence for order—they enjoyed very peculiar advantages for working out with wisdom and vigour the remedies which our times demand, and as if in them the grand language of the Prophet might be conspicuously fulfilled, 'They shall build the old wastes, they shall raise up the former desolations, and they shall repair the waste cities, the desolations of many generations.'"

Christian brethren, members of our great Public Schools, which we love better than our own lives, and which in the struggles, the sorrows, and even the bereavements of our manhood, revive and re-inspire the romance of our youth, has not this pious dream of seventeen years ago become, in large measure, a fact of our times? Has not the old spirit of the past *Noblesse oblige* been re-awakened in our day and at this hour to a second and a nobler life through the action, as I believe, of the spirit of the Cross penetrating and vivifying our ancient schools? He who was lifted up for the life of the world is still drawing all men unto Him, the hearts of the prosperous and the hearts of the young.

Only let us continue these hopes, these convictions, these works, under that same shadow of the Cross. Let us not suppose that faith in this crucified King, the Brother and the Lover of mankind, can be exchanged for any vague Christless philanthropy. God forbid that we should speak otherwise than with respect and sympathy of any efforts, whatever the motive power, to "remember the poor," and bring comfort and refinement to the homes of those who need both. But it is my profound belief that the fire of charity, as it was lit, so it can only be kept alive by the fire of faith; and that, apart from that deep personal devotion which the Cross of Christ inspires, philanthropy, or the love of the brethren—at least the love of individual brothers and sisters, often in themselves so repellent and uninteresting—would soon become, like eloquence divorced from charity, " a sounding brass and a tinkling cymbal."

Philanthropy in the abstract is one thing. It is, I suppose, the dower of all the larger souls, as it is the cant of the pettier. But the love of souls and bodies in detail, one by one, because they are the bodies and souls of brothers and sisters for whom Christ died, this is another thing. This is a plant of the "new creation." It is a lesson taught by no doctrines of man's teaching. It is learned at the foot of the Cross. Do you remember those lines of the poet,* when the poor nurse at the Hospital overhears some one whisper in scorn,

> All very well, but the good Lord Jesus has had His day?

She meets the taunt with little knowledge of history and none of philosophy, but with the instinctive logic of the heart and the Cross:

> Had? has it come?   It has only dawn'd.   It will come by-and-by.
> Oh, how could I serve in the wards if the hope of the world were a lie?
> How could I bear with the sights and the loathsome smells of disease,
> But that He said, Ye do it to me when ye do it to these?

Yes, brethren, there is much argument in that stanza. It is in the name of this Man, this mighty name which is above every name, which has no second and no third, that we of this Mission make our appeal. Without Him what would be zeal,

* Tennyson's Ballad, "In the Children's Hospital."

earnestness, eloquence, enthusiasm—nay, even heart to heart sympathy ; nay, even the proudest prestige, the gentlest refinement, the most fascinating charm of the oldest and dearest of our Public Schools ? It is while we work with Him, and for Him, and in His Spirit, and by His methods, for those whom He loves, that we may dare to receive His blessing—the blessing of Him the Crucified Sovereign of souls, who, even as we speak and listen, is drawing some men unto Him.

www.ingramcontent.com/pod-product-compliance
Lightning Source LLC
Chambersburg PA
CBHW032136230426
43672CB00011B/2353